Brand

How to market yourself in a competitive world

TIM FOSTER & MIA OLDENBURG

Studentlitteratur

Art. No 37761
ISBN 978-91-44-09272-0
First edition
1:1

© The authors and Studentlitteratur 2017
studentlitteratur.se
Studentlitteratur AB, Lund

Cover design: Francisco Ortega
Cover illustration: Shutterstock/Billion Photos

Printed by Interak, Poland 2017

CONTENTS

9 Managing Digital Brand YOU 161

10 The End is Only the Beginning … 179

AUTHOR INFO

Tim Foster is an award-winning teacher at Luleå University of Technology. With an undergraduate degree in Advertising from Michigan State University, as well as a graduate degree and doctorate from Luleå University of Technology in Sweden, he has over 25 years of teaching experience in branding, international business and international marketing. His work in academia has been within teaching, research and student recruitment, while also working as a consultant to companies and organizations around the world.

- LINK TO TIM: linkedin.com/in/timfos
- TIM ON TWITTER: @timfos
- E-MAIL TIM: timfos@gmail.com

Mia Oldenburg is Director of Student Affairs at Luleå University of Technology which includes the Career Center. In 2010 she was awarded "Pioneer of the Year" for her work at the university. She has a background in media and communication and has experience from a family business with several employees.

- LINK TO MIA: linkedin.com/in/miaoldenburg
- E-MAIL MIA: mia.e.oldenburg@gmail.com

CHAPTER 1

An Introduction to Branding YOU

"You don't find yourself – you create yourself."

UNKNOWN

This book is a voyage of self-discovery. Without turning this into a book on "branding" or "marketing", it is about taking some of the basics of what we know about branding and marketing and turning these ideas on to you, as though YOU are the brand. We then invite you to take this newly-discovered perspective on yourself to learn how to properly promote yourself and ultimately prepare yourself for the opportunities that are sure to come your way. This period of early 21st century social media makes it necessary to look at yourself as though you are a brand and take a new approach at a centuries-old phenomenon: *How do I get that job?*

This book is for many different types of people who are currently job-hunting or could and likely will be at some point in the future. Are you about to graduate from university, or for that matter, from high school? Are you currently unemployed or underemployed? Are you currently employed but want to find a new job and make a change in your life or give yourself a "fresh start"? Do you want to simply advance in the organization you already have a job with? Do you want to fight through difficult economic times or against increased competition for just about any job opportunity that comes your way? Do you want to take advantage of information technology and make nearly any region in the world your marketplace? Do you want to figure out what you *really* have to offer? If the answer to any of the above is *"yes,"* then this is the book for you.

The intent with this book is to K.I.S.S. (Keep It Short and Simple). It is not intended to bring into the discussion every theory or idea on branding or marketing, but instead use these often-misunderstood, and at times conflicting, concepts to turn YOU into a brand that becomes a more competitive consideration for the companies and organizations who are hiring during this early part of the 21st century. Today's hiring trends make finding and keeping a job a challenge, but if approached the right way, today's employee brand/employer brand "matchmaking" efforts will allow both sides of this core employment relationship to discover an array of mutual benefits, where both employee and employer win.

These are demanding times to be looking for a job and developing a career. Yet, in all honesty, most young people (university students, recent graduates), will embark on a life with many jobs and, potentially, multiple careers. Although not completely extinct, gone, for most people, are the days of working at the same organization and in the same job for 30–40 years before retiring. In the 21st century, the world is becoming your oyster, with the chance to look for opportunities both near and far. Opportunities that might lie within your areas of interest and connect to what you have been educated in, as well as opportunities that you never saw coming or knew could exist for a person with your background, education, or talents.

Today, organizations are not just looking for the right set of skills that help fill a vacant job opportunity. It goes beyond those items listed on a person's resume, or curriculum vitae (CV). Simply put, companies don't hire a résumé or CV – they hire a person. More importantly, they hire a professional yet personable *personality*. There are many people out there who have a good education, some solid work experience, and a few solid references. What is the difference maker? The answer lies within how you develop and market "Brand YOU". This book provides a roadmap for how to do this.

This is not the first or only book on personal branding and personal development. In fact, at times we will refer to some of the other books, as well as a few scholarly studies on personal branding, as these other authors have laid a foundation that looks at people as brands, or refers to what is a growing area of interest within employee (personal) branding and employer (corporate) branding. What separates this book from the others is that it not only provides a more holistic perspective on what makes you a "personal brand," but it combines this with a series of exercises at the end of most of the chapters. Put another way, this book is focused on being two parts *inspiration* to one part *perspiration*. You will get more out of the book if you both read and then work with the exercises at the end of most chapters.

While it is easy to see celebrities, sports figures, and politicians all as famous personal or "people" brands, the idea that *all* of us are brands is something fairly new. Therefore, connecting this idea to a more professional, streamlined strategy to create the career(s) and job opportunities that you want is a fairly new way of thinking. Before you start looking outward for that job opportunity, this book will make you look inward and discover and/ or reaffirm who you *really* are. It is only from this foundation that a true career strategy can evolve. Put another way, you have to know where you are now before you can develop a strategy to take you where you want to go at some point in the future.

The focus of this book is to build on these trends in personal branding and look at it from some additional perspectives, including the idea that this is not just a book to read, but in fact is a workbook as well. We don't want to tell you who you are; we want you to discover, create, and re-create who you have already become. We want you to consider yourself a "chameleon" of sorts, someone who is capable of change so that you can adapt to each job opportunity that comes your way or peaks your interest. And each opportunity is something that matches your specific set of skills, passions and professional interests. You as a brand must constantly seek to alter, improve, and develop yourself for each opportunity that presents itself in a lifetime that will likely be filled with a multitude of opportunities.

As already stated, both within and at the end of most of the chapters that follow this one, there will be specific exercises for you to take part in. It was Aristotle who stated, *"What we need to learn, we learn by doing."* For you as a brand this is vital, especially in gaining what we expect will be a different, more enlightened perspective on yourself, your talents, your interests, and where life can truly take you. While taking the time to do these exercises is entirely up to you, we can only say that doing them will provide a more solid foundation for you as a brand. It might also open your eyes to some windows of opportunity that you never knew existed before.

Reading this book, as well as taking part in the exercises we provide within and at the end of most chapters, does not guarantee employment. Instead, the aim is to allow you to find out more about who you really are and use this to increase the opportunities and reduce the risks that any brand faces in a competitive environment. For an example of an exercise, we have posed three general questions about you and the life you want (see

Exercise 1a at the end of this chapter). Such exercises will appear at the end of each chapter for you to work on as you read this book. It is recommended that you start a new Word or text document on your computer or purchase a notebook or diary where you can write the questions and your answers to them down by hand as you read the book.

This voyage of self-discovery may point you in the right direction, but it will not write your CV for you, let alone show up for that all-important interview. These vital tasks are on you, completely your responsibility. The aim of this book is to give you pause to consider the importance of such elements of communicating your personal brand. They might seem like "details" most of the time. But let's face it: There are many educated, experienced, skilled, talented, hard-working people out there. So, for the sake of argument, all of that being equal, then it must come down to the DETAILS we will discuss throughout this book.

At a minimum, we want to give you a few *"hmmm"* moments that make you stop and ponder and reflect for a moment. A *"hmmm"* moment simply provides an opportunity to deepen your thoughts on something you already knew about or at least think about something in a new way. However, we also hope you find a few *"A-ha!"* moments, which is when something that enters your mind will make you pause and welcome the notion that you have discovered or learned something new.

So as you read this book, please take your time. Re-read parts if needed. Stop and pause. Think. Then think again. Apply what is being written on the page to you by taking the time to work on the exercises made available at the end of each chapter. It is only from doing these practical exercises, in your own time, that the voyage of self-discovery can truly take place. Welcome to *Branding You: How to Market Yourself in a Competitive World.*

CHAPTER 2: What Makes YOU a Brand?

In this chapter, we will take a look at some of the more traditional viewpoints on what a brand actually is, and then turn that thinking onto YOU as the brand. Once we have established this, we will focus on providing you with a strategic look at developing yourself as a brand with Chapters 3–10.

CHAPTER 3: Getting to Know Brand YOU

Here we will cover what you need to know to truly analyze yourself and discover the current situation now facing YOU as a brand. What are your strengths and weaknesses that are deep within you? What are the opportunities and threats that lie outside your control that you need to take advantage of or find a way to deal with? This "SWOT yourself" approach allows you to answer one simple question: *What is the current situation facing Brand YOU right now?* You need to ask such a question for each and every job opportunity you face, as you are a dynamic, ever-changing personal brand.

CHAPTER 4: Matching Your Brand to the Demands of the Employer

In this chapter the focus will be on how to match your brand to the demands of the organization you are seeking employment with. The way in which human resource (HR) departments at many organizations, as well as the recruitment firms working for them, are organizing and implementing hiring practices, is quickly changing. Your relationship with the employer as a brand, as well as your ability to match your personal brand to the demands of the employer, is vitally important for each and every job opportunity that you seek.

CHAPTER 5: Setting Objectives for Brand YOU

While Chapter 3 looked at what the current situation facing YOU as a brand is, and Chapter 4 looked at the demands of the employer, this chapter will focus on helping you set objectives for Brand YOU. Where would you like to be at some point in the future? What specific goals have you set for yourself? What are your short-term versus long-term goals? What is/are your career objective(s)? And even more importantly, what are your life objectives? How can you make your goals SMART?

CHAPTER 6: Networking Brand YOU

Chapter 3 helped you look at where you are right now as a personal brand. Chapter 5 helped you set goals (where you want to be at some point in the future). What connects these two things is called STRATEGY, which is a "roadmap" to take you from where you are now to where you want to be at some point in the future. This strategy begins with taking a look at who you already know, then who they in turn know, and so on. Networking is about being genuinely interested in other people. The people you know and the people who they in turn know can open up more opportunities than you ever imagined. The key is first understanding then being willing to use your network to seek and at times create such opportunities for yourself.

CHAPTER 7: Communicating Brand YOU in Writing

This chapter will be about how to communicate your brand in writing, focusing on providing some tips on how to develop your written communication skills when it comes to writing cover letters, as well as tips on how to develop your curriculum vitae (CV), or, as some refer to it, the résumé. For consistency purposes only, we will refer in this book to such a document as a CV. It is amazing how many people never get the interview simply because they did not spend time thinking about the letter (or e-mail) and CV they have written and sent in. Even though many job offers come within your network, you will still often need a professional cover letter and updated CV for any type of job opportunity within or outside your network.

CHAPTER 8: Communicating Brand YOU in Person

This chapter builds on what Chapter 7 presented. If your cover letter and CV meet or exceed the expectations of the employer, chances are you will be called in for an interview. This chapter will focus on how to prepare for an interview and other formal and informal personal encounters that you will face when going for that next job opportunity. This chapter will present types of interviews and discuss what to expect and how to prepare for them. Both verbal and non-verbal forms of communication will be discussed, as well as interviews that could take place in person or via digital technologies such as Skype.

CHAPTER 9: Managing Digital Brand YOU

As we are well into the 21st century, how you use the Internet and all forms of information technology greatly reflects on you as a brand. Discussions on everything from social media such as Facebook, Twitter, and of course LinkedIn will be provided, as well as how to use Skype and other messaging interfaces for job interviews.

CHAPTER 10: The End is Only the Beginning

The end of this book is only the beginning of Brand YOU. This final chapter will act as a summary and focus on the end of the book being really the beginning to the "New & Improved" Brand YOU. This final chapter will go into how to handle Brand YOU during success, including tips on how and when to negotiate your salary, as well as how to handle your brand during times of failure. It will focus on taking what you have learned and done with this book so that you can begin to take the next step towards what we hope will be a truly "New & Improved Brand YOU."

Workbook – Chapter 1

In order to keep up with the Workbook portion of this book, we recommend you open a Word document or Notepad/text function on your computer, or simply purchase a simple notebook or diary/journal with blank pages of paper for you to write on. Nearly all of the chapters in this book will end with a series of questions/exercises for you to think about and answer. There are no right or wrong answers and we advise you do this so that the book on branding YOU connects to Brand YOU in a more direct and personal way. This first chapter has provided an introduction to Brand YOU. Below are some simple exercises you can do to connect to some of what was discussed in this chapter. These questions focus on asking you to consider some general issues regarding who you are before you go any deeper into the rest of this book.

EXERCISE 1 A – Answer the following questions

- Who inspires you the most? Why?
- Name three prioritized interests that you have right now. Why these?
- Why and how do I think I have affected people so far in my life?
- What kind of a person am I right now?
- What kind of a person do I really want to be?
- What am I the most proud of in my life so far?
- What matters most to me?
- What would I do if money were not an issue?
- What one thing would I do if I knew I would be successful at it?
- In general, what am I really good at?
- What makes me lose track of time?
- What do I like to do in my spare time?
- This is an example of a "success story" in my life so far …

- What is the "red thread" (connection) between my interests and my studies and/or work life/career right now?
- How do I show appreciation to myself?
- How do I show appreciation to others?
- How do I want to be remembered after I am gone?

CHAPTER 2

What Makes YOU a Brand?

"The most important asset a person has is his or her name."

DAVID AAKER

If you look at most marketing or branding textbooks, brands, historically, have been around for centuries, as it was a means to distinguish the goods of one producer from another. In fact, the word "brand" comes from the Old Norse word, *brandr*, which means "to burn" – like how we burn a mark into livestock still today.[1]

Today, a brand is defined by the AMA (American Marketing Association) as follows: *"A brand is a 'name, term, design, symbol, or any other feature that identifies one seller's good or service as distinct from those of other sellers.'"* The AMA definition goes on: *"A brand is a customer experience represented by a collection of images and ideas; often, it refers to a symbol such as a name, logo, slogan, and design scheme."*[2]

In fact, what attracts us towards (or repels us away from) a normal brand (company, product, service) is the same things that attract us towards (or away from) people. This idea that brands are like people is not new. As David Aaker, in his best-selling book *Building Strong Brands* writes: *"A brand personality can be defined as the set of human characteristics associated with a brand."* He continues, *"Just as the perceived personality of a person is affected by nearly everything associated with that person – including his or*

---

1 Keller, K.L. (2013), *Strategic Brand Management: Building, Measuring, and Managing Brand Equity*, London: Pearson Education Limited.
2 AVAILABLE: https://www.ama.org/resources/Pages/Dictionary.aspx (ACCESSED: September 2, 2014).

her neighborhood, friends, activities, clothes and manner of interacting – so too is a brand personality."

So while the idea that brands are like people has been around a while, the area of "personal branding" is fairly new. In a book called *Personal Brands* by Roberto Álvarez del Blanco, David Aaker in fact writes in the Foreword, explaining that the concept of a "person brand" might be new to most people, but we in fact have two brands to consider: Our professional brand and our personal brand. This book of course focuses more on the first of these, but as we will also argue, it is hard to separate the "personal" brand from the "professional" brand. Aaker continues: *"The most important asset a person has is his or her name and every person has a brand, represented by a name and face, that has a host of associated characteristics such as personality, interests, activities, friends, family, personal appearance, assets, skills and profession."*[3]

According to Shepard (2005)[4], personal branding and self-marketing consists of any number of activities that someone undertakes to make themselves known to the marketplace, generally for the purpose of obtaining gainful employment. According to Shepard, the start of personal branding dates back to an article by Tom Peters, who stated that we are all CEOs of our own company, a company known as "Me, Inc.", where the most important job you will ever have is to be the head of the brand called YOU! (Peters, 1997)[5].

We are continually reinventing ourselves and we work hard and long to build a solid reputation for our professional lives. Whether it is to take on a new challenge, shift into more meaningful work, or even in order to rebut perceptions that may have hindered our employability, taking control over your personal brand may mean the difference between an unfulfilling job and a rewarding career.[6]

---

3 Àlvarez del Blanco, Roberto (2010). *Personal Brands: Manage Your Life with Talent and Turn it Into a Unique Experience*, Palgrave Macmillan: New York.
4 Shepard, I.D.H. (2005). From Cattle and Coke to Charlie: Meeting the Challenges of Self Marketing and Personal Branding, *Journal of Marketing Management*, 21, pp. 589–606.
5 Peters, T. (1997). The Brand Called You, *Fast Company Magazine* (AVAILABLE: http://www.fastcompany.com/28905/brand-called-you; ACCESSED: March 30, 2015).
6 Clark, D. (2011). Reinventing Your Personal Brand, *Harvard Business Review*, 89(3), pp. 78–81.

So with this thinking in mind, if YOU are now the brand, then it becomes fairly straightforward: You too have a name, a "look", and most importantly, a distinct personality. While various aspects of each of these will be discussed in various parts of the book, we outline them here for you to consider right at the beginning:

- **Your name:** Like any brand strategy, you are trying to get that name onto people's tongues and make it both memorable and meaningful. The name should stand for something (positive). Avoid using nicknames, unless your nickname is something that you go by regularly. In fact, use the name that people call you by. Make sure you use this name, that your references use this form of your name, and that this form of your name appears (and is repeated) on written documents such as your résumé/CV, cover letters, business cards, etc. For example, your formal name might be Jonathon, but everyone calls you John. So use John Smith instead of Jonathon Smith on your CV, in your cover letters, and when introducing yourself. But if your friends from way back when continue to call you "Pooky", you might want to avoid using that kind of "cute" nickname. More on this in later chapters, especially when we present ideas on developing Brand YOU in writing (i.e. how to develop cover letters and CVs) in Chapter 7. NOTE: See Exercise 2a at the end of this chapter to work with this.

- **Your look:** You have a "look" that is derived from everything about your appearance. Your clothes and how you wear them; which colors work best on you in terms of your wardrobe; your hair and makeup; how you accessorize with watches, jewelry, piercings, etc. This will be covered more in later chapters as well, especially in Chapter 8 on communicating Brand YOU in person (i.e. preparing for interviews). However, it should be noted here that by "look" we do not mean whether you are tall or short or something to do with your body type. Instead, we are more focused on the non-verbal communication that revolves around dress code, accessorizing, and then of course body language and facial expressions. It is ultimately about how "Professional You" should have a thoughtful, professional look. By thoughtful, we mean that you have thought through what you are wearing and why. By professional, we mean that you have done your homework and adapted your wardrobe and look to the industry and organization you are trying to get hired by. NOTE: See Exercise 2 b at the end of this chapter to work with this.

- **Your personality**: You have specific personality traits that attract others towards you; you have other personality traits that repel people. It is this collection of personality traits that ultimately wins you the job or not. Simply put, your personality is a collection of strengths and weaknesses that define the very essence of your personal brand. NOTE: See Exercise 2 c at the end of this chapter to work with this.

Each of these elements of YOU as a brand will be discussed throughout the book. For now, the aim is to begin to really begin to understand yourself. Put another way, it's time to reaffirm what you already know about yourself or get to know yourself in ways you might not have done in the past. And if you think you really know yourself, read on ...

Your IMAGE vs. Your IDENTITY

While there is much discussion and even disagreement on what brand IMAGE vs. IDENTITY means within the general branding and marketing literature, for the purposes of this book, we will again borrow from David Aaker's *Building Strong Brands* discussion on these two concepts: A **brand identity** is what the brand owner or manager thinks of their brands (or how they want it to be communicated or perceived); whereas **brand image** is what others (customers, other stakeholders) think of the brand, or how it is actually perceived.[7] So based on this thinking, if YOU are the brand, then a simple way to look at this, your *personal brand identity*, is how you want to be perceived, which is often based on what you think of yourself. Your image is what others actually think of you. We will stretch this a bit further and for the purposes of this book state the following simplification:

---

7 Aaker, David (1996). *Building Strong Brands.* New York: The Free Press

- **Your personal brand identity**: What you think of yourself (often what you hope or want others think of you).

- **Your personal brand image**: What others actually think of you.

A true, generally more accurate strategy should be built on an awareness of what your image is, as there is often a mismatch between what we think of ourselves (or how we want to be perceived) *versus* how others actually feel about us. We will cover this in the next chapter.

In the branding textbooks, the use of brands revolves around one basic concept: *building brand equity*. We will use this to discuss how to apply this to building your very own personal brand equity.

Building your personal brand equity (PBE)

Brand equity has many definitions, but put simply, brand equity is the value of the assets of the brand minus a set of liabilities (Laforet, 2010)[8]. From a personal branding perspective, Vitberg (2010) explains that brand equity revolves around the building of a positive reputation.[9] This personal brand equity (PBE), according to Vitberg, consists of both tangible and intangible elements used to create value, as well as the relationships a person has built and maintained.

For our purposes, your personal brand equity (PBE) is really what the rest of this book will not only illustrate, but help you build and maintain as you read the book. Figure 2.1 below provides an overview of how PBE covers a wide array of tangible and intangible elements, organized as those elements you have control over versus those you don't.

---

8 Laforet, S. (2010). *Managing Brands: A Contemporary Perspective*. Berkshire: McGraw-Hill.
9 Vitberg, A. (2010). Developing Your Personal Brand Equity: A 21st Century Approach. *Journal of Accountancy*, 210(1), 42.

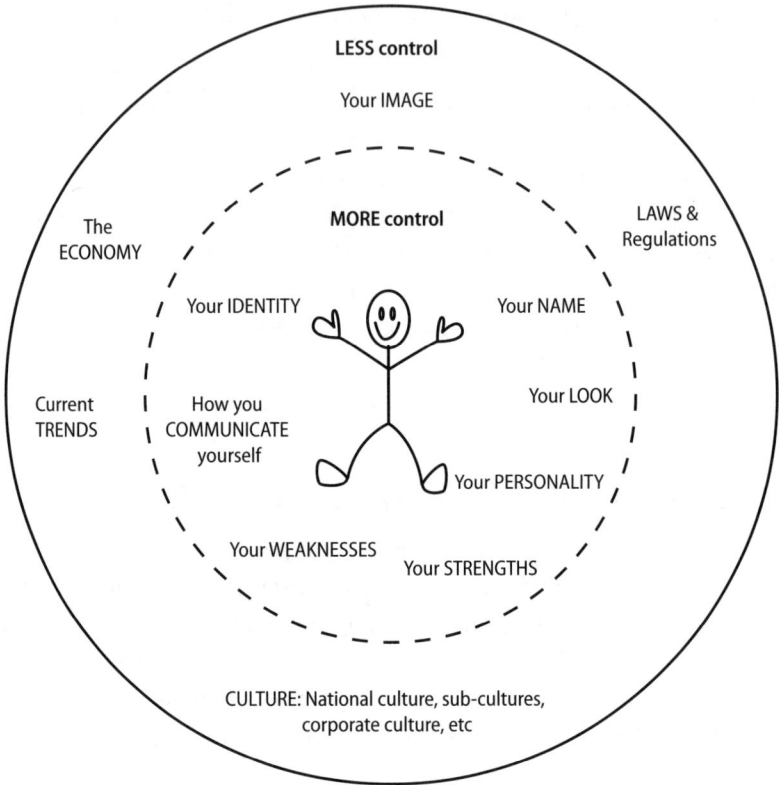

FIGURE 2.1 Overview of your Personal Brand Equity (PBE).

From Figure 2.1 above, you are dealing with both what you have no control over (e.g. culture, laws, trends, the economy, and of course what others think of you – i.e. your image – even though you can do things that affect how others feel about you). And while you are dealing with all of those elements, there are the areas where you do have at least some degree of control. These include your name, your look (e.g. your wardrobe), your personality (a collection of strengths and weaknesses), and how you communicate yourself. We will spend the rest of this book not only covering these issues, but doing so in order to help you build your PBE.

For now, please go back to your "notebook" (paper or on your computer) and remember to take a few minutes to take part in the practical exercises that connect to what we have just covered in Chapter 2.

Workbook – Chapter 2

This chapter has taken a brief look at what a traditional (product/service) brand is, what it means, and turned this thinking on to you, as though you are now a (personal) brand. Below are some simple exercises you can do to better understand some of what makes up YOU as a brand:

EXERCISE 2 A: Your name

Briefly describe your name, both first name and last name:

- What is the origin/meaning of your first and last names?

- How you feel about your first and last names?

- Are your names easy or difficult to pronounce and/or remember for others?

- How do you want others to refer to you?

- Do you think your first and/or last name(s) provide advantages or disadvantages when applying for jobs?

EXERCISE 2 B – Your look

Briefly describe your look:

- How do you feel about your overall look?

- Is there room for improvement in your overall look?

- What is your wardrobe style? What colors work best on you?

- Have you ever received a wardrobe consultation?

- How do you use accessories (jewelry, watches, piercings, tattoos)?

EXERCISE 2 C – Your personality (more on this in Chapter 3)

Before we take you into this more deeply in Chapter 3, provide a *preliminary* overview of how you feel about yourself vs. how you think others might think of you. Use both positive and negative words/phrases that describe you in these ways:

- **Your identity**: Briefly describe what you think of yourself. Use adjectives (words or short phrases) that describe you in both a positive and negative way.

- **Your Image:** Briefly describe how you think others see you. Do you think they see you in a fairly positive or negative way?

- **Matching**: How well do you think your IDENTITY matches (or does not match) your IMAGE?

CHAPTER 3

Getting to Know Brand YOU

"Our deepest fear is not that we are inadequate. Our deepest fear is that we are powerful beyond measure. It is our light, not our darkness, that most frightens us. We ask ourselves, who am I to be brilliant, gorgeous, talented, fabulous? Actually, who are you **not** to be?"

MARIANNE WILLIAMSSON

It all starts with self-awareness

The first step and most important issue in any professional setting is self-awareness. You should base your professional identity on your true self, your values, your passions and your dreams. This is what will give you the motivation to do what it takes to get the job, be it as an employee of another organization or as a self-employed entrepreneur. For some general questions regarding this self-awareness, see a series of self-assessment exercises at the end of the chapter.

You need self-awareness in order to base your career decisions on your own desires instead of basing it too much on other people's expectations of you. You need self-awareness when setting realistic but aspirational goals and when moving yourself towards those goals. You need self-awareness through the entire job-search process, including when writing your cover letter, your CV, and when engaging in that all-important interview. You need to be aware of your weaknesses so that you can avoid taking on work that will drag your energy down and tasks where you cannot perform at your highest level. However, your primary focus should be on developing your strengths and passions.

It is said that it takes 10,000 hours of practice (or 10,000 times doing something) to become really great at it. To keep the motivation going for 10,000 hours you need to, if not love, at least like what you are working on within those 10,000 hours. We are each given 24 hours a day, which adds up to 168 hours per week, generally around 700 hours per month, which means around 8,760 hours per year. The good news is that if you love what you do, you learn faster and perform better.

This means that, starting today, you can become a master of anything you set your mind to, no matter how you have used your hours before, as long as you are now willing to pay the price of 10,000 hours or doing something 10,000 times. And with only 8,760 hours per year, and the idea that you won't spend 24/7 on getting better at whatever it is you are working on, you have to be patient and give yourself time to improve in small increments, and along the way forgive yourself for making mistakes. Remember, mistakes are invitations to learn! Mistakes are invitations to get better at something over time.

While we are all born with certain talents, gifts or abilities, to keep those we need to practice. To get good at something we are not so talented or skilled in, we need to practice even more. Life, in fact, is a series of "practice" moments that add up to getting better or staying good at certain things.

When making such an inventory of your skills, remember to focus on and develop those skills that give you a positive feeling, what are referred to as "energizing skills." These are skills that should be conscious, developed, utilized and valued by you. An example of this could be writing skills: You like to write and "practice" this by keeping a diary, developing a blog, or writing letters to people you know.

Then everyone also has skills that are not as personally motivating, i.e. things you are good at but do not like to do. An example of this could include something like trying new things: You like it once you've tried it, but as a general rule you avoid these types of situations, as you prefer being a creature of habit. Try and focus on and utilize those skills that motivate you rather than those that do not, as a career filled with skills you enjoy using is often a richer, more rewarding career. However, always remember that true progress occurs when we push ourselves outside our comfort zones, at least once in a while.

Getting feedback from others is also important since you have skills that could perhaps be undervalued, undeveloped, unused or unspoken. These are skills that others see in you but maybe you do not recognize it as a skill yourself. Don't be so humble when others provide you with such positive feedback. Instead, thank them and then immediately ask yourself, *"Am I able to use such a skill I did not realize I had? If so, under what circumstances or job opportunities could such a skill be useful?"* An example of this involves **Sandra**:

> Imagine that Sandra suddenly received a compliment from a coworker on how well she organized an event for her company and what a natural she was at finding and leading others to help out in order to make this event a success. Since Sandra did not really see herself as a "leader" or "manager," such a compliment might come as a surprise. But within that compliment lies a skill or talent that others recognize in you that you might want to develop further in terms of a skill that many employers seek in those that they hire.

There are numerous ways of describing and categorizing people. There are several personality tests out there that you can come across in a job search situation, for example: Myers Briggs Type Indicator, 16 Personality Factor, BAS IQ, Kolbe, DISC, Personality Plus, Master Person Profile, Hogan's Personality Indicator, etc. Many employers will, in fact, use these to see what type of personality you are. And there are plenty of websites where you can try many of these tests to get a feeling of how they work and use them to prepare before an interview and learn more about yourself along the way. [1]

Different people are motivated and driven by different things. If you understand yourself better you will also understand others more (more on this in Chapter 4). Remember that a career does not have to be about moving up, it could be adapting your knowledge to a different field, building on your passion and interests, using your knowledge in a whole new way.

Malcolm Gladwell [2] describes different personality types that are needed in order to make an idea or product (a brand) tip over towards success (vs. falling back toward failure):

---

1 Simply do a Google search using the names of these types of personality tests for more information about what they involve and how you can take them.
2 Gladwell, M. (2000) *The Tipping Point. How Little Things Can Make a Big Difference.* Back Bay Books/Little Brown and Company.

- *Innovators* – the ones that come up with ideas
- *Mavens* – the expert that seeks to pass knowledge to others
- *Connectors* – "people persons" with a huge network
- *Salesmen* – make change happen through persuasion

Two basic questions for these personality types are put forth by Gladwell: Which one are you (even if you might be a combination of different types, you are likely to be "dominant" in one of them)? Do you know all of the other types within your network?

Everyone is probably a little bit of each one, but you really should reflect on which one(s) you are more of. Also think about what other people are expecting from or see in you and if this is what you really want for yourself? For example, do your parents expect you to choose a career as a manager when you in fact are driven by other things? Differentiating between what others want for you and what you truly want for yourself is important in your journey towards self-discovery.

The many layers of Brand YOU

One important aspect of being at your professional best when seeking a new job or career opportunity is to have an understanding of the layers of Brand YOU that go beyond only the Professional You that shines when you are trying to get that new job. As shown in Figure 3.1, there are three levels of your personal brand:

While Professional You is the primary focus of this book, i.e. the professional version of you that is made up of a collection of experience and education, abilities and skills, there is more to it than that. Ultimately, you have to be willing to manage three "layers" of Brand YOU, all of which should be considered and will be addressed in many parts of this book. These three layers of Brand YOU are Professional You, Personal You, and Private You. Remember, these three layers of Brand YOU are not mutually exclusive, so there is always some degree of overlap.

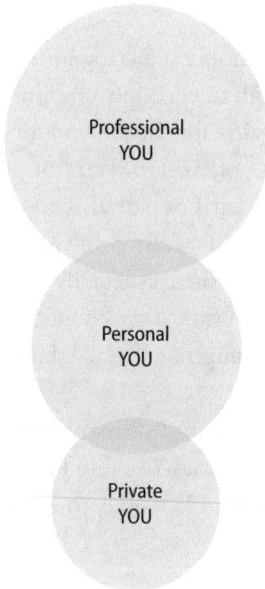

FIGURE 3.1
Professional vs. Personal vs. Private you.

LAYER 1: Professional You

This outer layer is the primary focus of what you share, online and offline, in writing and in person. Many different people in many different situations become exposed to this version of your personal brand. Professional You likely dresses differently, talks differently, and behaves differently than Personal You and more than likely Private You. It is the part of your Brand YOU that you want others to see and experience the most, especially in professional settings like in a job interview or at work once you get the job. Simply put, this is the most polished, perfected version of you. This is the you that comes through the second you leave your home every day, as you are constantly being observed once you do.

At this level, you are on your best behavior. You are dressed appropriately. You are always aware of what you are saying and how you are coming across to others. Companies and organizations hiring you want to know, and at times want to observe, how you handle stress, confrontation and authority. So they will test you on this before they hire you, often at interviews (see Chapter 8 for more on this).

LAYER 2: Personal You

With regards to Personal You we are simply referring to those elements of your *personality* that will come through in certain situations, both positive and negative, possibly while interviewing for the job and for sure once you are on the job. This layer shows that you are, in fact, not perfect and are allowed to have "bad days" and deal with personal issues, which is why this level overlaps with Professional You. It really revolves around how you choose to handle a bad day or personal issues, especially when you are in a public setting or on the job. More importantly, think about how the positive parts of your personality can shine through on "good" days and be tapped into on your bad days.

You can be a bit more vulnerable here, but you still need to be careful. There will always be some overlap of Personal You into Professional You, as you are who you are. However, this layer of Personal You can also overlap a bit with Private You as well.

LAYER 3: Private You

This is the innermost part of your brand, the intimate, private details of your life. This is the layer you need to be the most careful with. This does not imply you have deep, dark secrets. It simply means that there are likely certain elements of your life and your personality that you want to keep just that – private! There is of course overlap with Personal You, so parts of this layer will come forth in professional setting once in a while.

A good rule of thumb: Within the walls of your own home is your private life. However, what happens the second you walk out of your home, elements of Personal You (i.e. your personality) are on display for others to see, interact with, and respond to. From this vantage point, a good way to think about it is: The closer you get to work, the more important it is that Personal You becomes Professional You. We of course share private details with our closest friends at work; we of course can have vulnerable moments where we get upset or lose our temper. But remember the golden rule of communication: *It never matters how we intend something, it only matters how someone else can take it.*

In today's social media world and 24/7 news cycle, nearly everyone you pass on the street is some sort of pseudo-journalist – ready to report something funny, weird, or controversial. They can do this by posting it on their Facebook page, Tweeting it with a photo or video on their Twitter page, uploading it to YouTube, or writing about it in their blog. Gone are the days of higher levels of anonymity that came with living and working in the 20th century. In today's 21st century, we are on display the minute we walk out the relative safety of the private place we call home. Put simply, once you step outside the front door of the place you call home, you are vulnerable and on display. We will cover this more in Chapter 9, *Managing Digital Brand You.*

However, for those of us living in a smaller town, the overlaps within these three layers of Brand YOU frequently become even more blurred, while elements of your personality will always shine through as Professional You connects to Personal You. Overall, the advice here is simple: As often as possible, Professional You should mix with those parts of Personal You that highlight the best parts of your *personality.* Everything else, whenever possible, you should try and leave at home with Private You.

In a very traditional and conservative industry there might not be room for too much personality, so it is often strictly business, and professionalism is expected at all times. However, even though your target market is mainly interested in what you can do for them *professionally,* they are also looking for a person with a nice *personality* to work with.

While there are many personality types out there, and many tests to take to see what type of personality you are, we have borrowed a traditional way to learn about yourself as a brand. Companies do it (with their brands), so why shouldn't you do it, since YOU are the brand? We call this, "SWOT Yourself".

SWOT yourself

Businesses and brands that work with developing a strategic plan connect two opposite poles based on two very simple questions: *Where are you right now?* (What is the current situation facing the company/brand at this point in time?) *Where would you like to be at some point in the future?* (What are the specific, measurable objectives of where you would like to be at some point in the future?). What connects these two poles is something called STRATEGY, which will be covered in the chapters following this one.

So before you can develop any specific, measurable goals for yourself as a brand, let alone develop the strategy needed to reach those goals, you first need to know where things stand for you as a brand right now, today, and usually for each new job opportunity. We are, after all, dynamic, ever-changing beings. This will be done through a few, suggested self-discovery exercises that will allow you to discover things about yourself you never knew, or maybe some of them you do know, but this will help confirm it. More on this at the end of the chapter in the Workbook section for this chapter.

You are an imperfect being; an imperfect brand. There are positive and negative aspects within you that you control; there are those things outside yourself that you can't control but that you need to find a way to deal with (as outlined in Chapter 1 on creating your PBE – or personal brand equity). In business, we call this a SWOT analysis, which stands for *Strengths, Weaknesses, Opportunities*, and *Threats*. Every brand out there, corporate brands, product brands, and service brands alike, must deal with these internal and external factors. Since you are now the brand, so do you. Let's look at each part of the SWOT individually:

- **Strengths**: Parts of ourselves that are positive, that we have at least some control over, and that we should be taking advantage of.

- **Weaknesses**: Parts of ourselves that are negative, that we have control over, and that we should see as "what to improve on" rather than any sort of failure. Remember, there are weaknesses that can be "spun" in a positive way as opposed to those that are not so easy to "spin" out of (an example of this is provided in a few pages).

- **Opportunities**: Those things outside ourselves, that we have no control over, but answer one question: What is out there that we can take advantage of in our careers?

- **Threats**: Those things outside ourselves, that we have no control over, but answer questions such as: What is out there that we are afraid of or intimidated by? What can get in my way of getting hired?

Strengths & Weaknesses

To further expand on the above four areas, for a company or a brand, *Strengths* and *Weaknesses* come from within the organization; it is what the brand owner/manager has at least some degree of control over. Strengths are something to take advantage of. Weaknesses are something you have to get rid of, go around, or somehow deal with strategically.

However, remember that your Strengths and Weaknesses can be described from two perspectives. Like so many companies and brand managers, strategy is often built upon the brand IDENTITY, as we discussed in Chapter 1. As a reminder, the brand IDENTITY is what the brand owner thinks of their own brand; brand IMAGE is what others think of the brand – and you should always build strategy on what your image is!

Therefore, when attempting to "SWOT yourself" as a brand (see the exercise for this at the end of this chapter), what are some *Strengths*, or positive aspects of you (your personality) that you can take advantage of? What are some *Weaknesses*, or negative aspects of Brand YOU, that you need to overcome, improve, or at least find a way to deal with?

An example of the power of using this "SWOT Yourself" exercise to discover your strengths and weaknesses comes to us from a student who took part in one of our first versions of the course "Branding YOU" at Luleå University of Technology in Sweden. As this individual developed her positive IDENTITY adjectives (what she thought of herself), one of the ways that she described herself in a positive way was that she considered herself "funny" or having a good sense of humor – she thought she could make people laugh.

However, she soon found out that her identity, or what she thought of herself, did not really match up all the time with her image, or what others thought of her. After talking to others about what they thought her Strengths versus Weaknesses were, from both those who knew her personally and those who knew her on a more professional level, "funny" never came up as a Strength. In fact, she discovered that her sense of humor was not really considered funny at all, as, "funny" or "sense of humor" or "humorous" never came up when others described her in a positive way. However, in looking at her Weaknesses according to others, "negative," "sarcastic", "a bit dark" came up. Was it possible that when she saw herself as "funny" or having a "good sense of humor," others took her sarcastic humor as something negative?

In reflecting upon this rather startling identity vs. image conundrum, we asked her: *Why do you think you missed this? How could something you saw about yourself as being so positive, a real strength, actually end up being something that others saw in you in a negative way, or as a Weakness?* The student explained that this pushed her to really think about how she came across to others. A few weeks went by, and we met her again. We asked if she had come to any conclusions. Answering yes, she went on to describe, in an extremely honest way, that what she thought was funny, was instead seen by others as "whining" or negative because her humor was more often than not a bit sarcastic in tone. She felt that others perhaps laughed either out of embarrassment for what she was saying or making fun of, or simply because they perhaps felt obliged to "laugh along" with whatever was said.

This was a real eye-opener for her. It became something that she said she would absolutely remember, not only for interviews, but in those small talk situations in both business and even her personal life where a bit of humor can help break the ice. She talked openly about how much it hurt to discover this about herself, but how glad she was that taking the time to "SWOT" herself made a difference in not continuing down the path where what she thought was one of her greatest Strengths was ultimately a fairly big Weakness.

Opportunities & Threats

Outside Brand YOU there is the world of the unknown, the unpredictable, and the uncontrollable. There are cultures out there that we have no control over. There are competitors trying to get that same "dream job" who we can't do anything about. There are corporate policies that dictate hiring practices and job requirements. There are laws we have to follow and rules that will guide us. There is technology and the economy. Opportunities and Threats are those things outside ourselves that we have no control over, but we need to find a way to deal with them: Take advantage of those Opportunities we want to invest our time in; somehow deal with the Threats that face us and are always changing.

Common opportunities that often affect your career or chance at certain

36

job opportunities might include the economy: in stronger or improving economies, organizations are hiring; in weaker economies, they are not. Technology is perhaps the 21st century's biggest proponent for career advancement: We are using information technology to find jobs, as well as at times employers finding us (see Chapter 9 on *Managing Digital Brand You*).

A sample SWOT

Let's illustrate the use of "SWOT Yourself", and let's use a fictional character by the name of **Lukas**:

Lukas feels he knows himself well and is aware of how others feel about him. He wants to find employment within the IT industry and has a dream of working for a company (or starting his own) dealing with the development of apps for smart phones. Below is an example of what could come up when he SWOTs himself for just such an opportunity:

STRENGTH for Lukas: Creative. That one word is how others often describe him and he feels this about himself as well. He would like to find a job where the right side of his brain, where creativity resides, is challenged. He knows his left-brain "logic" will take care of itself.

WEAKNESS (negative example): Late. According to those who know him, Lukas has a habit of arriving late and making others wait. Why is this a bad example to use in a job interview? Because there is no way to "spin" out of this weakness. "Spin" is the art of taking something negative and turning (spinning) it into something positive. Companies don't hire "late." While this is something Lukas needed to get better at, it is not a weakness he wants to admit to in a job interview (and yes, they will likely ask him in an interview what he considers a weakness or two to be); nor does he want any of his references saying this about him – and yes, they will ask your references about your weaknesses as well.

WEAKNESS (positive example): Stubborn. It is easier to spin out of this, as stubbornness in an individual can often allow them to say that this means they finish what they start; they often exceed expectations; they can handle more than one thing at a time. Flip the stubborn coin and you have the strength, Driven or Determined.

OPPORTUNITY: Information Technology, and more specifically digital technology, has generally followed Moore's Law – the idea that computing power doubles every 18 months. This is exciting, as it means what was not possible today might be possible in a few years. Lukas appreciates that what he can be creative about today will be vastly different in just a couple of years. This more than anything else is what Lukas wants to take advantage of but has no control over.

THREAT: The economy. The economy has been weak both globally and where Lukas lives and would like to remain at this stage of his career. Bad or uncertain economic times can mean companies are not hiring or are even cutting back. There is nothing Lukas can do about the economy – unless moving to another city, region or part of the world would be of interest, so long as the economy in that part of the country or world is that much better.

While SWOT answers one question: *What is the current situation facing the brand (that would be YOU) right now?*, objectives (what we cover in Chapter 5) look at where you would like to be at some point in the future. Strategy (Chapters 6–9) is what connects these two anchor points.

However, before you can start developing specific objectives for yourself, let alone a strategy, it's a good idea to learn from how this understanding of YOU as a brand will match or connect to the expectations of the employer. Therefore, the next chapter is about matching your brand to the demands of the employer. However, please remember to take part in the practical exercises we provide for Chapter 3 first, which start on the next page.

Workbook – Chapter 3

This chapter has focused on getting to know Brand YOU. When it comes to strategy, you need to understand the current situation facing the brand (where am I now?). Then you set specific objectives (where you would like to be at some point in the future). What connects these two "anchors" is strategy. Below are some simple exercises you can do to begin to take a comprehensive look at the current situation facing you as a brand right now.

EXERCISE 3 A – Good vs. Bad?

Take a few moments to think about the following two questions with regards to your Skill Inventory within the context of getting hired for most job opportunities.

- In general, what am I already good at (skills/talents/abilities)?
- What do I need to get better at?

EXERCISE 3 B – What motivates you?

Which of these motivates you more (put an X before each one that applies):

_____ Being in charge (you are driven by deciding, having responsibility for others)

_____ Achieving high goals that I set for myself/have been set for me

_____ Being the expert

_____ Trying unrelated things

_____ Having work/life balance

_____ Taking risks, having an adventurous life

_____ Feeling free and independent

_____ Having routines and feeling safe

EXERCISE 3 C – Self-assessment exercises

the following four exercises will allow you to form a self-assessment across several career-related topics. In the end, there will be a summarization table for you to fill in what you circle in each of the following four self-assessment exercises (i.e. interests, values, industries, and attributes).

INTERESTS: What do you like to do when you are working? *Circle the things you like to do in your daily career* (feel free to add new words):

Problem solving	Coordinating	Packaging
Questioning	Editing	Transporting
Collaborating	Documenting	Managing machines
Networking	Counting	Mediating
Reinventing	Caring	Categorizing
Developing	Interviewing	Negotiating
Designing	Making an inventory	Summarizing
Marketing	Writing	Purchasing
Building	Organizing	Predicting
Reviewing	Evaluating	Preserving
Assembling	Producing	Leading
Working with strategy	Providing service	Repairing
Explaining	Communicating	Budgeting
Researching	Building teams	Entertaining
Arranging	Coaching	Being active
Exploring	Teaching	OTHER: _____
Analyzing	Selling	
Consulting	Keeping track of things	

From the list above, prioritize and define the 3–5 most important INTERESTS that you have for yourself – why are these the most important?

VALUES – What are your career values? What is important to you in career-related situations and what values do you want others to associate with you? Circle the values that are most important to you in career-related situations (feel free to add new words):

Job-satisfaction	Fairness and trust
Influence	Self-expression
Helping others	Clarity
Results	Intellectual stimulation
Privacy	Predictability
Participation	Promotion
Recognition	Rewards
Income	Leadership
Altruism	Aesthetics
Job variety	Status
Morals	Competition
Flexibility	Authority
Passion	Independence
Meaningfulness	Prestige
Creativity	Public attention
Competence	Peace and quiet
Networking	Accuracy
Friendship	Entrepreneurship
Achievement	Adventure
Development	Risk taking
Work/life balance	Communication
Responsibility	Job stability
Job security	Informality
Teamwork/cooperation	OTHER: _____

From the list above, prioritize and define the 3–5 most important VALUES that you have for yourself – why are these the most important?

INDUSTRIES – Where do you want to be working? You can always pair whatever education you have to the industry that interest you. Be creative and think about how you can add your passion and your education to find different areas for you to be working in. For example you could be an accountant working in the fashion industry. *Circle the industries and sectors you like to work in* (feel free to add your own words):

Finance/ Banking	Travel/Tourism	Human Resources/ Recruitment
Safety/ Security	Artistic (illustrating/ painting/sculpture)	Music
Interior design	Theatre/Film	Healthcare
Politics	Beauty & hair	Education
Media/ Communication	Fashion	Photography
Insurance	Audio technology	Advice/Coaching
Electronics	Hotel/Restaurant	Telecommunications
Gardening/ Floral	Real estate	Retail/Commercial
Building/ Construction	Archaeology	Law
Child care	Sports/Wellness	Research
Military	Publisher/Library	Design
Transportation/ Logistics	Agriculture/Forestry	Chemistry/Physics
Production/ Manufacturing	Animal care	Biotechnology
Architecture	Computer/IT	Business
	Advertising/ Public Relations	Environment
	Events/Conferences	Technology
	Diplomacy	Export/Import
	Social sector	OTHER: _____

From the list above, prioritize and define the 3–5 most important INDUSTRIES that you would like to work in – why are these the most important industries for you?

ATTRIBUTES – Which words describe your best attributes as a person?

Circle the words that you think fit you best (feel free to add your own words):

Loyal	Self-starter
Committed	Strategic
Honest	Balanced work/home life
Enthusiastic	Ability to deal with pressure
Reliable	Extrovert/People person
Common sense	Creative
Sense of humor	Flexible
Motivated	Good self-esteem
Adaptable	Organized
Resilient	Cooperative
Proactive	Confident
Driven	Self-discipline
Responsive	Tactful
Methodical	Open-minded
Focused	Doer
Inspiring	OTHER: _____
Decisive	

From the list above, prioritize and define the 3–5 most important ATTRIBUTES that you have for yourself – why are these the most important ones for you?

SUMMARIZING your self-assessment: Go back to each of the four self-assessment exercises you just completed and look at what you prioritized at the end of each exercise. What are your interests, values, interests, attributes and industries? Then use these key words to reflect and then summarize what you need in your career in order to be at your best.

Prioritized INTERESTS:	Prioritized VALUES:

Prioritized INDUSTRIES:	Prioritized ATTRIBUTES:

Using the words above, reflect on what could become some of your future career choices:

EXERCISE 3D – What is important to you?

Take a few minutes to think about (and perhaps write down) what is important to you in your career:

- Do you want to be the expert in your field or do you prefer to be challenged by learning new things?

- Do you want to be someone who is in charge or are you better as a teammate?

- Do you want to widen your area of knowledge or are you better off staying more focused within one area?

- Do you have the will to try completely new things or are you more comfortable with routine and being that creature of habit?

- What is your orientation?

- Would you describe yourself as **action-oriented** (i.e. demanding, impatient and dominant); or are you more **people-oriented** (i.e. inspiring, outgoing, lively)?

- Do you think you are more **routine-oriented** (i.e. loyal and patient); or are you more **detail-oriented** (i.e. accurate and critical)?

EXERCISE 3E – SWOT Yourself

In this exercise, you will actually "SWOT Yourself." Follow these steps to give it a try:

- **Uncover your identity:** Write down 8–10 positive things about yourself. Another way to look at this is to describe yourself using 6–8 positive words or short phrases. Then write down 6–8 negative things about yourself (areas of yourself that you are trying to improve). This is your IDENTITY (how you see yourself, or how you hope others see you).

- **Discover your personal image:** Call or meet in person 3–5 people that you know more personally (family, friends). Try and use a mix of younger/older, male/female. Ask EACH of them separately to state

3–5 positive things about you (words or short phrases describing your *Strengths*). Then ask them to tell you 3–5 negative things (nothing too personal – just things they think you could improve regarding your personality (these will be your *Weaknesses*).

- **Discover your professional image**: Then do 3–5 separate interviews with people you know on a more professional level (past or present coworkers, bosses, people you have volunteered with or did projects with in school). Again, a mix of male/female, older/younger, if possible. Ask them the same two questions: 3–5 positive things they feel about you (again, these are your *Strengths*) and 3–5 negative things/areas for improvement (*Weaknesses*).

- **Analyze**: Compare your identity (what you think of yourself, both positively and negatively), with your image (what others think of you, both positively and negatively). Is there a pattern (similarities and/or differences)? Then, within your image (what others think of you), are there any patterns (similarities and/or differences)? How does Personal You compare to Professional You? How do you compare to males vs. females? Younger vs. older?

- **Opportunities**: Write down 3–5 things that are outside your control that you would like to take advantage of when it comes to your career. Examples of this could include information technology, an improving or strong economy (somewhere specific, perhaps). You don't control these things, but they are there for you to take advantage of to help your personal brand.

- **Threats**: Just as you did for Opportunities, only these are things outside your control that are negative. Another way to look at this is: *What are you afraid of* that is outside of you and your control? A weakening economy (less chance to get hired), perhaps where you are currently living, is just one example. Another example would be if you wanted to work in sales but needed to be able to use your car to travel and oil prices kept going up, making gasoline for your car more expensive.

CHAPTER 4

Matching Your Brand to the Demands of the Employer

"Customers buy for their reasons, not yours."

ORVEL RAY WILSON

Getting to know the company or organization, the type of industry they are in, as well as the people in such an organization, is the only way to start your journey towards becoming employed. Simply put: *do your homework!* If you are one step ahead and know that you are someone who can solve a problem or add something of value to an organization in the job opening that a specific organization is offering, then you have a competitive advantage. Know that employers hire for their reasons, not yours. So understanding their reasons and needs to fill a specific job opening is vital for you before you even begin to update your cover letter or CV for that specific job opportunity. One of the biggest mistakes people make is that they don't adapt/update or connect their cover letter and CV to what the job advertisement is describing. Too many people use the one-size-fits-all model and send out the same cover letter and CV for all job openings they might be interested in.

Instead, focus on matching your cover letter, your CV, your social media profile, and *yourself* (should you get an interview) to the requirements of the organization providing a particular job opening that you are interested in. It all begins with reading the job ad carefully – what words are they using? Who are they really looking for? Then go online and learn more about the organization and industry this job will be in. Then go back to your cover letter and your CV (both of which will be covered more in Chapter 7, *Communicating Brand YOU in Writing*).

In your letter, you really need to match your brand to the demands of the employer you are seeking to obtain employment from by really reading

4 MATCHING YOUR BRAND TO THE DEMANDS OF THE EMPLOYER

the job ad and using some of the words they are using to describe what they are looking for and use those same (or similar) words in your letter. Of course you do this only if you feel you really have those attributes, skills or strengths. You can also connect to how you describe yourself on your CV using some of these words. If they are looking for a person with certain traits, and you write about other traits than those in your letter and/or CV, then you are only communicating that you are not a match.

Furthermore, if you are able to match or come close to what they are looking for, your CV can also demonstrate to them that they might need your expertise or talents, even if they are not looking for that at the moment. Job opportunities are not only offered by employers, but can be created simply by the experience and skills of a potential employee. Although our focus is on matching Brand YOU to the demands or needs of the employer, more than one job opening has been created by simply getting your CV in front of them to demonstrate they might need other skills as well.

As a new graduate, or even when you are still a student, you might think, *"Well hey, someone needs to first give me a chance to learn the business before I can start to solve their problems!"* Of course, the branding then should really focus on you showing great interest in the business, your motivation to learn, and your ability to become a top performer.

Attitude is everything

To get an insight into the mind of the hiring manager, put yourself in their shoes. One hiring manager[1] put it like this:

> "What do employers really want? People who can create a difference even in tough situations; people who are able to deal with instability; people who think of solutions instead of problems; entrepreneurs that never give up & work in teams; people with ambition, courage, passion and curiosity; people who seek opportunities and who can define achievable goals. Attitude is everything!"

---

1 Ana Gonçalves, Unilever, lecturing at ISCTE Business School (January 22, 2014).

While none of us are all of these things, the point of what this hiring manager is saying is simple: We are looking for someone who has at least a combination of some/most of these abilities.

Analyze the company you are interested in working for as a part of an overall target market. How can you help solve their current challenges? How can you help them reach their goals? How can you contribute to their success? You need to get to know the business and the people in the industry and ask relevant questions to find out if you are a match with such an organization, or at least how you can become a better match in the future. An example of this uses the fictional character of **Jack**:

> Jack was keenly aware before he went into the job interview that this new start-up company where he was invited for an interview was more focused on the products it was developing than on the market those products would serve. If there is one thing he learned in business school, it was that a company's mission should always focus on the market, not the product. The professor who hammered this home to his students made a lasting and valuable impression on Jack as he completed his degree in Marketing. So many of the courses he took at university were focused on applying what they were learning in real-life situations. This allowed Jack to realize he really had something to offer this company he was going for an interview, before the interview took place.

Transferable Skills

Every brand that is successful has specific target markets that it matches up really well with. So knowing your target market when YOU are the brand is just as critical. And based on this, you need to be able to market yourself and match your brand to the demands of the employer brand. In the end, this comes down to being clear about your *transferable skills* (see the exercise at the end of this chapter for you to evaluate your transferable skills). Transferable skills are skills you can use in a variety of jobs in a variety of industries. These types of skills include such things as: communication skills; people skills; teamwork skills; problem-solving skills; analytical skills; management/leadership skills; time-management skills; organizational skills; etc.

If you are currently pursuing a university (or even high school) degree, take the time to reflect on what each course and each professor or instructor is actually trying to teach you. Too many times students in high school and college focus on what they have to do to pass the course rather than on what they will learn or gain from taking that course. In addition to the actual content or focus of the course (i.e. why is it required for your degree or why did you choose it as an elective course), what is it giving you in terms of developing other skills that are often transferable to any job setting? What should you focus on instead? What is an individual course doing to develop your *people and communication skills*? Your *analytical and problem-solving skills*? Your *organizational and time-management skills*? How about your *leadership/management and teamwork* skills?

Keeping track of what you learned from such environments can also give you something to offer in terms of an example in a job interview. Finally, how will these classroom experiences match what the particular employer you are interested in might be looking for? You need to know going in to that interview, in a clear and articulate way, why you specifically want to work for that organization. A lot of times this is about connecting your cover letter, CV and answers in your interview to the job advertisement that listed what they are looking for. Other times it's about offering them something they didn't know they needed but that you possess.

Small improvements in yourself can have a great impact on your career and every career starts with being employable, meaning the ability to be hired due to your being a more attractive brand for the employer than other brands (candidates) who are vying for that same opportunity. Being employable means you have the ability to:

- **Obtain**: Get a job within your competence range
- **Achieve**: Perform in that job and deliver results
- **Develop**: Advance within that job/organization
- **Adapt**: Change jobs; seek other opportunities

But employability can also be measured in skills and attributes that all employers are looking for in their recruits, regardless of educational background. Being self-aware, having networking skills, and knowing what gives you meaning and what you need in order to perform at your best are just some of the attributes listed by employers. So work to keep your competencies fresh and up-to-date. Be open to change and be ready to adapt. Passion, communication skills, cultural understanding, problem-solving skills, people skills, learning ability, ethics and analytical thinking are also often on the employers "wish list" regardless of, or in addition to, what the specific job requirements might be.

These *transferable skills* are pretty much needed in all jobs and are skills you should attempt to develop during your years at high school, university, trade school, or just having various jobs in your earlier years (i.e. if you are not going to university). Either way, you work to continue to develop these during any facet of your education and/or career.

You do not need to have all of these transferable skills, nor do you need to be equally strong in all of them. In fact, don't feel overwhelmed if you don't see yourself in all of the attributes listed above. They are just some examples of some of the more typical attributes that employers are looking for – what they are looking for, regardless of who they are hiring. Keeping up with developing yourself by following thought leaders within these areas, going to conferences, and your courses and lectures, should always be seen as adding value to Brand YOU. Not everything is fun or entertaining, but you should always be able to find value in everything you do, be it learning through school or learning through experience.

Included within these transferable skills are *employability skills*, which can be divided into three categories, all of which employers are looking for and expecting of you professionally:

- **Educational knowledge** – your degree and what you have learned by completing it. IMPORTANT: Always finish your degree and get that piece of paper in your hand! Most people make the mistake of only focusing on educational knowledge while undertaking the job search process. There is actually so much more to you than just this, as described above.

- **Transferable skills** – communication skills; people skills; teamwork skills; problem-solving skills; analytical skills; management/ leadership skills; time-management skills; organizational skills.

- **Personal attributes (from Chapter 3)** – being loyal, enthusiastic, positive, motivated, trustworthy/reliable, hard-working – remember, *attitude is everything!*

In a 2012 alumni career survey[2] of graduates from 2008 and 2009, conducted at a university in Sweden, alumni were given a list of 15 intended learning outcomes and asked to rank which ones were required in their every day job on a scale from not at all to very much. The following were most required on the job regardless of their field of study:

- Teamwork/cooperation
- Solving problems independently
- Critical thinking
- Explaining to non-specialists
- Making presentations/communication skills
- Being part of business development
- Following the knowledge development in their respective field

How can you develop these skills and build a strong CV that shows employers that you are competent in these areas even if you lack extensive work experience? If you are currently a university student, it really is quite simple: *Get involved!* Take the opportunity to join, volunteer and work with any number of on-campus or off-campus organizations for students. If you are not a university student, the same thing applies to you at other levels of your education. If you are not in school at all, then getting involved might mean volunteering for a non-profit organization or helping out at community events that interest you.

---

2 From the Swedish university report "Time Before and After the Exam", a study done by the Career Center at Luleå University of Technology, Sweden in May 2013. (Tiden före och efter examen – en karriäruppföljning av alumner som tog examen vid Luleå tekniska universitet 2008–2009" LTU Karriär 2013-05-20).

Different personality types are needed for different kinds of jobs. And you need to identify the key skills for Brand YOU for each job opportunity you seek. As said before, but worth repeating, this also means you need to not only know yourself and know which of your transferable skills and personal attributes stand out and can be communicated, but you also need to know your target market, i.e. the demands of the employer, in order to make sure your personality and skills fit their organization and team. Most importantly, you cannot focus only on your educational background when branding yourself. Your transferable skills and personal attributes are just as, and at times, even more, important.

It is estimated[3] that one-third of the recruitment undertaken for a single job opportunity fails. There can be many reasons for this: Maybe the "right" candidates didn't apply for the job opening. Perhaps the job description and salary level need to be changed in order to attract the right type of applicants. In some cases, it might be that the wrong person is hired and is unable to actually perform what was expected of them.

So who is the "right" candidate then? And what does it mean to be competent? Of course organizations want to hire people with knowledge and the theoretical educational background they are looking for in the particular job opening. However, they also want people with the skills to put theory into practice; the ability to perform at a high level; and the willingness to go the extra mile and be someone to exceed expectations rather than merely meet them. Ultimately, it is really a combination of many attributes that make up the "ideal" or at least "right" candidate for any one job opening, as shown in Figure 4.1, The Competence Puzzle.

---

3 From a presentation by the Swedish business organization, Svenskt Näringsliv (2010), a study among 60,000 member companies, Linköping, Sweden.

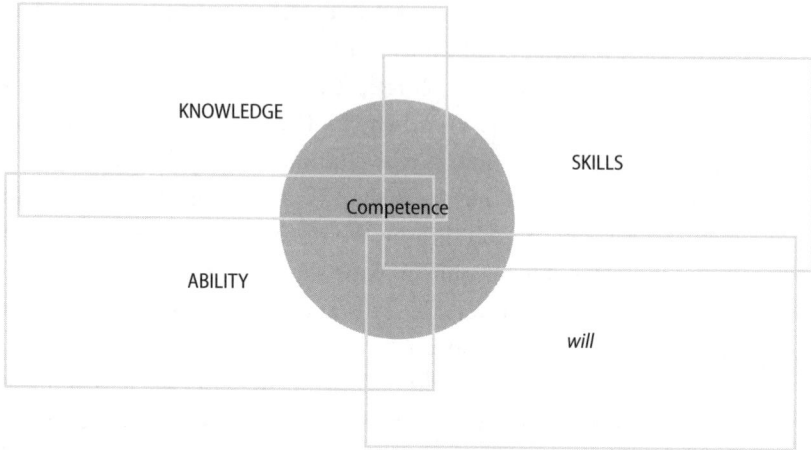

FIGURE 4.1 The Competence Puzzle that is your true value proposition. (SOURCE: Adapted from Svenskt Näringsliv presentation in Linköping, Sweden, 2010.)

As shown in the Competence Puzzle above, it is where KNOWLEDGE, SKILLS, ABILITY and WILL overlap that competence truly exists. It is what your true value proposition towards the employer becomes. Your education alone does not equal competence. Too many people, especially newly-minted college graduates, often think it is primarily about this. Although it plays an important role, there is so much more to a "competent you" than just your formal education.

Your Knowledge

Don't think of your education, or degree, as being the proof you need that you are competent and capable of doing the job. Your education simply implies you should have a strong working knowledge of a particular area of study. This education is not only theoretical but hopefully has certain practical elements as well, providing current knowledge within your particular area of study. Your education also shows that you have the ability to learn. And that is what employers want you to continue to be able to do once they hire you. In fact, going to school is really about just that – *learning how to learn*.

That being said, we hope you paid (or are currently paying) attention in class and use your university or other educational opportunities in life to really absorb information and become more knowledgeable. For so many students, the college (or other educational) experience is more about the social-cultural benefits of this type of investment of your time. And it is just that – an investment. Too many college (or even high school) graduates go into their first job interviews as they near graduation regretting not having worked harder, paid more attention, or focused more on why they really put themselves through the educational experience in the first place, which was to learn. Simply put, it is highly advisable that you treat any educational opportunity as probably the most valuable investment you will ever make in yourself.

Your Skills

In addition to your education, you also need a set of very specific **skills** that the employer will be looking for, and such skills often come from previous work experience, voluntary work, or things you have been involved with in the past. It is not all of your skill sets that will be in demand, but this is about you matching your skills to what the employer is looking for. And it is never just the skills that an employer may be looking for that pertains to a particular job description. While not important for all jobs, many of today's job opportunities call for other skills that are not specifically taught as a part of your college major. Such skills could include:

- **People skills:** Your ability to interact and deal with people from a variety of backgrounds in a multitude of different situations.

- **Communication skills:** Your written, verbal, and non-verbal communication skills.

- **Analytical skills:** Your ability to process large amounts of information and make sense of that information in limited time. Then using this information to make intelligent, informed decisions.

- **Emotional skills:** The ability to identify and manage your own emotions and the emotions of others. This is generally said to include three more specific skills: Emotional awareness, including the ability to identify your own emotions and those of others; the ability to harness emotions and apply them to tasks like thinking and problem solving; the ability to manage emotions, including the ability to regulate your own emotions, and the ability to cheer up or calm down another person.[4]

Your Ability/Abilities

Ability is yet another requirement for the fully competent Brand YOU. While many believe that skill is the same as ability (and we agree they are not mutually exclusive), ability focuses more on how well you use your knowledge and skills over time, at a high level, and in a variety of settings. Ability focuses on using your knowledge and skills in stressful situations and with a variety of people. Some people can use their knowledge or a skill in only a single setting or within a specific context.

An example of this is an athlete. A quarterback in the NFL generally has the ability to analyze large amounts of information within seconds of being exposed to a certain situation (e.g. the defense they are lining up against when it is 3rd down and 15 yards to go). The skill that can come from that is connected to what he might do after his playing days are over, for example working as a stock analyst on Wall Street, where analyzing large amounts of information within certain time constraints is a sought-after skill in that industry as well.

Your Will

Even your **will** (your *will*ingness to get the job done) is only one piece of the competence puzzle. Are you motivated to complete the task at hand? Are you actually disciplined enough to get the job done? So much about will is really about your motivation to actually reach your goals.

In an interview on the CBS news show "60 Minutes", American football coach Nick Saban, from the University of Alabama (and former head coach of the Michigan State Spartans), stated something that revolves around three

---

4 AVAILABLE: www.psychologytoday.com/basics/emotional-intelligence (ACCESSED August 30, 2016).

simple words: **DO YOUR JOB!** Coach Saban expects this of himself, as well as everyone who works for him. The point of this example? Coach Saban has the *will* to show up every day and work hard, to do the job necessary to develop and maintain a winning football program. His expectation is that everyone else on the team, including players, coaches, equipment and film mangers, administrative staff, even the person who cleans the offices at night, are all willing to do the same.

This epitomizes the idea of being a part of the team. Being a good teammate generally requires three things:

1. **Time:** Show up; give of your time.

2. **Effort:** With that time, add something of value to the team; use that time to provide something valuable to the effort; actually work to move towards results.

3. **Positive attitude:** You need to contribute your time and effort, but no one likes working with a jerk. You need to stay positive while doing the first two items on the list.

It is the combination of knowledge, skills, abilities and your overall *will*ingness (determination) to do your job that adds up to your competence for any one job. And doing that job rests on the fact that you do indeed show up and do what is expected of you … and as always, a little bit more.

Is it really about education and experience?

Another way of looking at what has been discussed above is the simple formula that so many job seekers seem to go by:

$E + E = O$
Education + Experience = Opportunity

The more or the higher the level of education that you obtain (high school degree … associate's degree … bachelor's degree … master's degree … doctorate or professional degree), the more opportunities will open up under that level of education, and the levels that preceded it. Put another way, a diploma is like a passport – it allows you to journey to places you never knew existed until you earned the right to do so.

However, education is only the first half of the formula. Experience is the other half. Nearly all job opportunities require some degree of experience. But experience does not always have to come only from other jobs you have held. Those voluntary activities also count. The key is staying busy, even when unemployed. Experience can mean other paying jobs, but it can also mean giving up your free time to help at a homeless shelter; helping out at the Red Cross; coaching a group of young people in a sport at your local community center or local school; taking the time to teach or share a talent you have (singing, playing an instrument, juggling).

Experience is built on a foundation of waking up each day and choosing to do something constructive for ourselves, but more importantly for others. In fact, it comes down to a more advanced formula than just E + E = O. In this example, motivation is added to the mix.

$$(E + E) \times M = O$$
(Education + Experience) × Motivation = Opportunity

Motivation x the value of Education + Experience takes this discussion on what you want to do each day to an entirely new level. Many recruiters often use this type of formula in order to rank the applicants for specific job opportunities. Let's say the applicants are given a value from 1–10 on each of these three areas: motivation; education; experience. As you can see in the formula, motivation is the most meaningful since high scores on that will dramatically give you a higher total score even if you are not the most experienced applicant or have the highest educational background. On the other hand if you are NOT motivated for the job, it does not matter how much education or experience you have. You will fall flat in the process. Being motivated and having the willingness to do a good job is nearly always ranked *very* high by employers.

But what is motivation and how do we find it inside ourselves? According to Robins and Judge (2009), motivation is the process that accounts for an individual's intensity, direction, and persistence of effort toward attaining a goal. They go on to explain that *intensity* is about how hard a person tries;

direction has to do with working towards beneficial goal; and *persistence* is about how long a person tries to obtain that goal.[5]

Motivation is one of those words that is used a lot, but not always truly understood. It's easy to be motivated when things are going well, but many times we take that sort of positive momentum for granted. And what about those who are working to overcome heavier obstacles in life or who don't have the same opportunities as others to begin with? Whether overcoming obstacles or taking advantage of opportunity, in the end, it is up to each individual to find something deep inside that makes them motivated. What is it that makes us willing to overcome obstacles and create opportunities for ourselves? As discussed in the previous chapter, self-awareness should help you find that motivation and passion.

However, regardless of whether you come from a background filled with opportunity and privilege, or one filled with obstacles and challenges, motivation is something we still need to find within ourselves. Motivation is not something you can give, teach or sell someone. The only thing you can do is facilitate the process of someone finding the motivation they need inside themselves. In fact, those from less-privileged backgrounds, who have had to struggle, are often more willing to work hard and sacrifice. They simply know what it takes to push through and get things done. And regardless of your background or circumstances, there are certainly things in your life that you are proud of. What have you accomplished so far in your life? What is there left to accomplish?

However, let's build a scenario around two people using this simple formula of $(E + E) \times M = O$:

Example: Marcial vs. Emily

Let's say there are 100 people interested in a job opportunity offered by a company. Out of 100 cover letters and CVs that come in, approximately 50 will go in the "no chance" pile. Out of the remaining 50, perhaps 30 will go to the "Maybe, but we'll get back to these CVs" pile. The remaining 20, plus perhaps another 10 from the "Maybe" pile, end up in the group that is

---

5 Robbins, S.P. & Judge, T.A. (2009), *Organizational Behavior*, Upper Saddle River, NJ: Pearson Prentice Hall.

invited for a first interview. NOTE: Out of those 20, around 15 (an estimate) were already known from the network of the employer or recruiter, which is how they got a head start in the race for the interview before it even started.

These 30 candidates, after their respective first interview, most likely with a recruiting firm or someone from Human Resources within the company, may be narrowed down to 10 final candidates. These Top Ten are then invited to a second interview, and this group is then narrowed down to two finalists for that job opportunity. Out of those two finalists, the M × (E + E) becomes very important, as motivation is a personality trait and comes across in how you express yourself in an interview.

For the sake of a fictitious example, let's take each of these two finalists and run some fictional numbers to give you an example of who is more likely to get the job. The following is the case of **Marcial** vs. **Emily**. Look at how motivation has such a large impact for each of them and the circumstances they face going after the same job at this company.

> **MARCIAL:** On paper, Marcial is the ideal candidate. He has a degree from a top university, excellent overall grades and a near-perfect GPA (Grade Point Average – which is an important issue in some job opportunities in those cultures where grades are calculated on a numerical basis). He has also accumulated some excellent work experience, specifically related to the job he is seeking. His experience includes both paid positions (i.e. work experience) and other activities where he volunteered his time and talents (i.e. additional experience). So using the first formula above, he received a 9.5 for his education; for his experience he received a score of 8.5, bringing it to a total E + E score of 18.
>
> But when it comes to motivation, there was something missing. He came across as a bit too nervous and unsure at the interview. He wanted so desperately to impress his interviewers that he appeared to be needy and a bit desperate – too focused on his exclusive education, excellent grades, and substantial experience. And, worst of all, he failed to show interest in the company and the position he was being interviewed for. He thought his degree, where he obtained it, and the grades in the courses that made up that degree were everything. His score for motivation was put at a meager 5.0.
>
> MARCIAL'S SCORE: (9.5 + 8.5) × 5.0 = **90**

EMILY: Emily comes from a smaller, relatively unheard of university. She received a good education and ended up with average grades and an average GPA. Nothing spectacular, but she passed her courses and finished her degree. She worked part-time while at school, selling shoes at a sporting goods retailer at the local mall. Going after the same job opportunity on the basis of education and experience, Emily's education and experience make her virtually a no-chance candidate on paper. Her score for education is a very average 6.5; her score for experience a bit lower, only 5.5, for an E + E score of 12.

However, she had just enough on her CV to be invited for the job interview. When she got to the interview, Emily dazzled them all. She was well-spoken, extremely confident (without coming across as cocky), and seemed at ease with answering whatever questions they had for her. She also showed great interest in the position and the organization by asking intelligent and well thought-out questions that showed she was focused on how she could provide the best value for the employer. As she had a personal interest in this field of business, the interview turned into more of a dialog rather than Emily just answering questions. When asked about her less than stellar grades and limited experience, she gave them the honest answer they were looking for: That her work schedule often had her working evenings and weekends, providing limited time for sleep and studying, but this was the only way she could afford to have an education. Emily's motivation score was a strong 9.0.

EMILY'S SCORE: $(6.5 + 5.5) \times 9.0 = \mathbf{108}$

So, who gets the job – Marcial or Emily? Having enough on your CV regarding education and experience is important. But the key is getting into the interview, which is the only place where motivation via your attitude and personality can be demonstrated. This is why no one is ever really hired directly from their CV (although many organizations make this mistake – they hire CVs, not people). And more and more, organizations don't simply hire people, they hire personalities. Showing that you have a real interest in the company will make them interested in you. And getting them to like you is the first step to getting a job offer. However, while 20% of your success will be based on WHAT you know, 80% can be based on WHO you know, which will be discussed more in Chapter 6, *Networking Brand YOU*.

Ultimately, while what you have accomplished in your professional life, such as your education and/or your work experience, is important, it is also becoming more and more about what kind of person you are, i.e. your personality. Your attitude, motivation and passion need to fit what the organization hiring you is looking for. A lot of it has to do with how motivated you really are for the job you are applying for. While many have desires or "wishes" to accomplish things and reach their goals, motivation is the hard work and sacrifice that is given up along the journey that takes you toward that goal. Then once you reach that goal, what do you do with it?

Now that we have looked at what the current situation facing Brand YOU is (Chapter 3) and what the demands of the employer can be (Chapter 4), we move on to setting objectives for Brand YOU (Chapter 5).

But before you get started with Chapter 5, make sure you look at a few practical exercises that will help you with regards to what was just covered in Chapter 4.

Workbook – Chapter 4

This chapter has focused on matching your brand to the demands of the employer. It builds on and connects directly to what was discussed in Chapter Three, which focused on getting to know Brand YOU. In the exercises below, you are being asked to reflect on yourself from the perspective of what employers are looking for – or to match your brand to the demands of the employer.

EXERCISE 4 A – Take a moment and think about two people you know:

- Ask them to tell you about their jobs.

- What knowledge, skills, and abilities do they need to do that job?

EXERCISE 4 B – Find 3 different job ads you are interested in:

- Carefully read what they are looking for.

- Do you have what they are looking for? How can you demonstrate that? If not, how can you make yourself a better match? What do you need to do?

- Match YOUR brand to these three potential employers. What are your *transferable skills* that would fit all three (see Exercise 4 c below for some examples)?

EXERCISE 4 C – What are your transferable skills?

Employers are looking for a variety of skills, regardless of your background, education or experience. Nearly any type of job in every industry is looking for a collection of many of the skills listed below.

Circle those skills that you feel you possess that are truly transferable, i.e. you can call upon them regardless of the job opportunity.

Communication skills	Mediating/negotiating
Teamwork skills	Selling skills
Problem solving skills	Critical thinking skills
Taking initiative skills	Development skills
Planning/organizing skills	Budgeting/economic skills
Self-management	Entrepreneurial skills
Learning skills	Coaching others
Technology	Sustainable and ethical thinking
Leadership/management skills	Language skills
Service skills	Analytical skills
Drive/motivation skills	Representing skills
	OTHER_____

CHAPTER 5

Setting Objectives for Brand YOU

"You were put on this earth to achieve your greatest self, to live out your
purpose, and to do it courageously."

DR. STEVE MARABOLI

Have you ever heard of the dancer and musician Phyllis Sues?[1] In April 2013
she turned 90 years old and she is loving life. However, she was not always a
dancer and musician. She actually did not become one until she was in her
70s. She believes everything is possible, which is why she started a fashion
label in her 50s and began practicing trapeze in her 80s. She truly is living
proof that you are never too old and it is never, ever, too late to set new
objectives for yourself and change your life around.

What you believe in matters and Phyllis Sues most certainly believes in
her ability to achieve whatever she wants, regardless of her age. How long
do you expect to live? The possibility that you are NOT yet finished with
your life and still have a lot of time ahead of you to make change is very high
unless you are a lot older than Phyllis.

In Chapter 3, we discussed the current situation facing Brand YOU. We
gave you exercises to discover more about yourself than you ever thought
possible: From general, reflective questions to trying to "SWOT Yourself."
All of this worked together to answer the question for Brand YOU: *"What
is the current situation facing you right now?"* In this chapter, we will take
the current situation facing Brand YOU, together with what the employer
is looking for, from the previous two chapters respectively, and then move

---

1 AVAILABLE: www.huffingtonpost.com/phyllis-sues-/aging-gracefully-phyllis-sues-yoga-
tango_b_2878155.html (ACCESSED: May 22, 2016).

© THE AUTHORS AND STUDENTLITTERATUR

65

forward and help you to develop objectives for your career. This focus on future Brand YOU will also focus on one, simple question: *"Where would you like to be at some point in the future?"*

If Chapter 3 focused on where you are right now (with Chapter 4 presenting what employers are looking for), and this chapter focuses on where you would like to be at some point in the future, strategy (starting in the next chapter) will allow you to focus on connecting these two poles. **Strategy** is the roadmap that connects where you are now to where you would like to be at some point in the future. **Tactics** are what you do along the way (hour-by-hour, day-by-day, week-by-week, year-by-year).

But what kinds of objectives should you set? Is it only about your career, or is it also (more) about life and what you want to accomplish with it? These days, especially thanks to information technology, our work life and personal life are becoming more and more intermingled. So much about what we want to do in our lives is either directly or at least indirectly connected to the jobs we have and the careers we develop. This chapter will help you focus on two primary objectives: Your *career objective* and your *life objectives.*

As with dividing your identity into professional, personal and private, so too can you do with your objectives. You will of course have *private objectives*, such as wanting to find the love of your life. Perhaps settle down and get married? Maybe one day have children? Perhaps you would like to quit smoking? Maybe drink a little less on the weekends? Perhaps exercise more and lose some weight? These are all private objectives.

You also likely have some *personal objectives*, or objectives that connect more to your personality, or how you are as a person. There are always those parts of our personality that need improvement: Perhaps you want to be *stronger* in saying no more often; there might be a part of you that has the goal to be *nicer* to those who call you on the phone to sell you something. Then there are always those parts of personality that focus on the positive aspects of your personality: Maybe your goal is to use your abilities to be so *focused* and *determined* to get even more done in your life and in your career; or what about using your *energetic* personality to volunteer more often.

Ultimately, especially now in the 21st century, when we are so connected to everything through information technology, our work life is not mutually exclusive or disconnected from the lives we lead at home or when we are not at work (more on this in Chapter 9).

Your private, personal and professional objectives need to build upon each other just as your short-term objectives need to support your long-term ones and ultimately help build your vision for the future. Otherwise it will be very difficult for you to achieve any of them. Your vision can be thought of as a "perfected image" of your future. What do you want your life to be like down the line? What you do day-to-day should ultimately lead up to that desired future.

The focus in this book is primarily on helping you develop your *professional objectives*. It is good to think of this as both short-term and long-term. Examples of this include a short-term objective like updating your CV, or getting called in for an interview based on that CV. A long-term example would be actually having that interview turn into a job offer and starting that new job!

Knowing your *Strengths & Weaknesses* (as a part of your "SWOT Yourself" exercise in Chapter 3) will help you become successful and choose wisely for your future. You will go after the *Opportunities* that are right for YOU. Understanding your limitations and focusing on your strengths does not mean limiting yourself in any way but rather helps you keep a positive, aspirational but still a realistic outlook on your future. If you can give yourself a clear answer as to WHY you want to achieve the objectives you have set for yourself you will build the motivation needed to see it through. If other people are dictating your goals you might end up feeling unfulfilled no matter what you achieve, or worst case, you might end up not getting anywhere at all.

Having realistic expectations for your life will also help you increase your self-respect. Having a life plan that is too hard and contains unrealistic goals often produces the exact opposite. You need to be able to see the top of the mountain when you are climbing it, and once you have reached it you will set your standards even higher, but you will not be motivated if you feel that the top is too far away and you can't even see it.

While trying to reach the top you need to be open-minded enough not to miss opportunities along the way or become so stubborn that you keep banging your head against a brick wall trying to obtain a goal that is completely out of reach. However, this should also be balanced with not giving up too early, as there will be obstacles (or threats) along the way that you have to deal with as well. This balance between striving for your goals for too long or for not long enough or just long enough is not easy. Let your common sense be your strongest guide.

Being self-aware also means you have to be honest with yourself if the desired results fail to emerge. This is where you should distinguish between dreams that can be completely unrealistic and lack a timetable and objectives that are more concrete and clear, where you can see the steps you need to start to take in order to be able to someday achieve them. The steps needed should be fun or at least worthwhile. Not everything might be described as fun, but you can often at least find value in what you are doing to achieve your goals. It is simple to reason that the more fun you are having, or at least the more value you are finding in what you are doing, the more likely you are to follow through to the end. At least make sure you understand that there is something, in the end, that you will gain by doing what is necessary to reach your career and your life goals.

Setting SMART Goals

Building your objectives on this foundation of self-awareness provides you not only with a high level of motivation, but also with a sense of its meaning. This in turn leads to a positive attitude and often greater than expected results. Unrealistic self-expectation leads to stress and self-blame (or blaming others) for the lack of results, and creates a negative attitude, which generally leads to reduced productivity.

It's really about being SMART about your goal-setting. The SMART model is very useful when setting goals and will help you formulate your goals so that they are easier for you to reach. To be SMART, your goal needs to be: **S**imple & specific, **M**easurable, **A**ttainable, **R**elevant, and **T**imely.

Each one of these SMART objectives is discussed in more detail, providing both a weaker version of an objective vs. a stronger one that could be made. You need to fit this to those SMART objectives you come up with for your career (see Table 1 for some simple examples of setting SMART goals).

TABLE 5.1 Creating SMART Objectives

SMART objectives:	WEAK:	STRONG:
Simple & **S**pecific	Become rich	BETTER: Save money BEST: Save $50/week
Measurable	Save as much as I can	Save 10% of my take-home pay each month
Attainable	Win the lottery; become a millionaire	I can afford to save (or invest) $200 per month
Relevant	"Save for a rainy day" or "Just in case"	Save towards a specific goal for you or your family (education, car)
Timely	I will do this "When I get a chance" or "When I can"	I will do this each month; I will do this by a specific date

Having clear and SMART objectives is just the beginning. To actually reach your goals you also need *courage* to go after what you want and courage to tell the right people where you want to go and how they can help you get there. You need *knowledge* within the field you strive for and you need to have a *network* of people in the business you are interested in. You also need to strongly *believe* that you can achieve what you have set out to do, because if you doubt yourself others will too. With courage, knowledge, a solid network and belief in yourself, you will have an easier time getting where you want to go.

There are some goal-setting traps that almost everyone reaches at some point. Sometimes you just see too many roads ahead and you might feel that it's hard to start moving in any direction at all. Having too many options can often halt your progress towards any goal. To help you structure your alternatives and help you move from ambivalence towards a decision, there is a simple model for structuring your situation (see Figure 5.1):

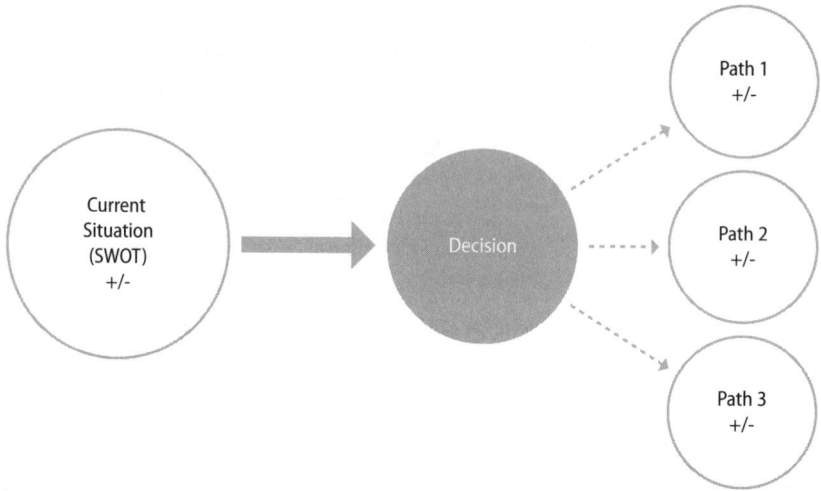

Figure 5.1 Structuring alternatives for Brand YOU.

From Figure 5.1 four specific steps emerge:

1. Describe your current situation by looking back at the "SWOT Yourself" exercise you did at the end of Chapter 3.

2. Describe your alternatives and the positive and negative outcomes (or the pros and cons) of each path and ask yourself: What can you gain with each path? What can you lose? What would your life look like 5 years ahead should you choose this path? Further down the road? Are there roadblocks ahead? Are these alternatives really my own or is someone influencing me?

3. Pinpoint when you need to make your decision. Is there a deadline, maybe a deadline for applying for a job or a school?

4. Figure out how to get there. Getting from where you are now to your target, and breaking your goal into smaller pieces and steps (what are called tactics) that are easy to take will prevent you from feeling that it's impossible to reach.

Strategy is the roadmap that takes us from where we are now (our current situation) to where we want to be at some point in the future (reaching specific, measurable objectives). And there can be many routes or paths to follow. Tactics are what we do along that journey when following the roadmap. This means that progress comes in small, sometimes tiny steps. You have to see the specific, small steps that you take each hour, each day, each week, etc., as proof that you are moving forward toward those objectives. Let's use the example of **Sarah**:

Sarah is about to graduate from a major university with a degree in social science. Upon looking at her current situation (Sarah conducted a SWOT on herself), she has a decision to make: "Do I take my degree and begin my career, or do I continue with graduate school and potentially go on and get a Ph.D.?"

Path 1 for Sarah was to get her degree, leave university, and begin to apply for jobs. This had various advantages (make money now) and disadvantages (give up goal of going to grad school). Her goal was always to get a degree and begin to work, but her love of learning and the idea of working towards a master's and possibly even a doctorate really materialized as she got closer to completing her undergraduate degree.

This means that a new opportunity, or Path 2, emerged. The idea of this path is to stay in school and continue work on a master's degree in sociology and use that as a springboard toward possibly completing a doctorate and stay within academia as a career, or move out to industry with more advanced degrees. One advantage for choosing this is she gets to do what she loves – study and learn! The disadvantage involves going into more debt as she continues as a student taking student loans to pay bills.

Her third option, Path 3, was perhaps her most viable: Continue part-time with graduate school as she took a job that allowed for flexibility for her studies, but the job was related to her chosen field. The advantage was obvious, the best of both worlds! One disadvantage was the toll this could take on her, as going to grad school (even part-time) while holding down a full-time or even part-time job was extremely demanding. Depending on which path she chose, there were certain steps (tactics) she needed to take care of the day after making that decision ... then the week after ... the month after ... and so it goes.

Building Momentum

If you want to be at a certain point within a year, where do you need to be in 6 months? In 3 months? A month from now? A week from now? By tomorrow? What small step do you want to start with today? That first step is always the most difficult. It is amazing what happens when your first step turns into more steps and this turns into something magical called momentum.

While looking at where you are at now is simply a starting point, what ultimately matters in reaching your goals is what you decide to do from this point forward. Look at someone else who already reached their desired target: How did they get there? Can you walk in their footsteps? Can you use the same path as they did? Getting a mentor to help you along the way is invaluable, and many times a mentor is someone who has simply accomplished what you are interested in accomplishing. You not only see where they are now and what they have accomplished, but you benefit from understanding what it took for them to get there and how they did it.

Keep in mind that if you already know *exactly* how to reach your goals, then they are likely not big or bold enough! The "bushel full of apples" is perhaps helpful here: Almost anyone can eat an entire bushel of apples if they do it over time and eat just one apple at a time, one bite at a time. However, no one can open their mouth and empty an entire bushel of apples into their mouth. The lesson here: Focus on the smaller pieces that you can chew and before you know it, you've reached your target. It's the old cliché of learning to take things one step at a time.

Mapping alternative routes, or roadmaps, as well as being flexible and ready to adapt along the way, will give you even more power and momentum to reach your goals. Be brave enough to change your direction, or take another route, if the one you're on doesn't lead you where you want to go. Maybe you are doing hard work in the wrong direction. Take ownership of your situation and look ahead. After all, it's your life, so changing your mind, going in a new direction, or "flip-flopping" is perfectly fine, so long as you are doing what is best for you.

Other pitfalls and traps when setting objectives, besides seeing too many alternatives or being indecisive about them, can include: Setting too many goals at one time; not really focusing on the ones you have set for yourself; not really deciding that this is truly what you want to do; not basing your objectives on what you really want but on what others expect from you; giving up too easily (sometimes even right before the finish line); not giving yourself a realistic amount of time to achieve your goals or setting an unrealistic timeframe; getting stuck planning and discussing things rather than acting on them; or setting goals that contradict one another. What you should do is simply be strong enough to continually evaluate the roadmap you begin to follow, and change your route or direction if you have to.

As Walt Disney famously said:

"The way to get started is to quit talking and begin doing."

Another way of looking at this, from hockey legend Wayne Gretzky:

"You will always miss 100% of the shots you never take."

Some of you reading this might argue that you don't want to miss out on opportunities, so why set goals at all? Why not leave it all up to chance or coincidence? You also might claim that there are plenty of examples of people who have succeeded without setting goals and without planning their careers. Of course there are these exceptions. In fact, many of the opportunities that will come into your life you never saw coming or set as a goal.

However, setting goals can help you become even more successful. Have you ever heard of a regular brand or company not setting goals then not developing a strategy to achieve those goals? They might be out there, but most (successful) companies know what they are facing right now, then set goals, then create strategies (and undertake tactics) to help them achieve those goals.

Having specific, measurable objectives gets you moving and motivated. You can always change direction over time, but being stuck and letting weeks, months, or even years pass you by, waiting for chance or some coincidence to occur is likely not the most constructive way to develop Brand YOU.

Managing chaos

However, even if you set goals, the world is a chaotic, unpredictable place at times. As Wheatley (2006)[2] points out, chaos theory can be applied to our careers. She explains that the world is far more sensitive than we ever imagined, since the world around us acts in a non-linear fashion. This means that small changes can have great impact if repeated over time. In contrast, big changes can have little to no effect at all. What this means is that luck or chance will occur, including both good luck and bad luck, because in this chaotic world we live in, there are just too many variables outside our control.

Putting it another way, one of the most famous scientists of our time, Stephen Hawking, once said: *"Intelligence is the ability to adapt to change."* So set objectives for yourself, but remain flexible and be prepared to adapt as things move forward. Remember, when you did the "SWOT Yourself" exercise in Chapter 3, those things outside your control, called Opportunities and Threats? The existence of these forces simply means that you might suddenly need to face things outside your control. None of us have a crystal ball – so be prepared and be ready to adapt as you follow your roadmap, or the strategy you develop to achieve specific goals.

Being persistent and having the willpower to follow through with your goals, no matter how hard it seems, is yet another factor for success. History is filled with people who had to struggle for years to convince others of their idea, never giving up and finally reaching the desired success. And what about people having to face others putting them down, saying they could not amount to anything, then proving them wrong and then used that as fuel to reach their goals. A good example of this comes from Thomas Edison, who said, *"I have not failed. I've just found 10,000 ways that won't work."*

History is also filled with other people whose lives did not go according to plan no matter how hard they tried. But can you ever truly fail? From our perspective, a person does not fail. Your life may not always go according to your plans because of unexpected challenges. And luck (or the lack of it), i.e. those things you don't control, will also play a part at times. But you are never a failure and should never see yourself that way.

---

2 Wheatley, Margaret J. (2006). *Leadership and the New Science: Discovering Order in a Chaotic World.* San Francisco: Berrett-Koehler Publishers, Inc.

Choose to look at life as a series of experiences and learn from everything that happens. Learn, gain experience, be flexible and adapt your plans. The ability to recover from setbacks is incredibly important in order to achieve your goals. If you erase the word failure from your thinking, you stop being afraid to try. Take all your past "failures" and think about what you learned from these experiences instead and you can then turn it into a unique set of strengths. *Mistakes are invitations to learn!*

To summarize, it really comes down to a never-ending cycle of adapting yourself to each and every job opportunity, following the same steps that companies and brands all over the world follow:

1. **SWOT Yourself:** Just like we asked you to do in Chapter 3: What is the current situation facing YOU as a brand at this particular moment, for this specific job opportunity?

2. **Set SMART objectives:** If SWOT is where you are now, where do you want to be at some point in the future? What are some specific, measurable (i.e. SMART) objectives for you to work toward? And as a part of this, understand the demands of the employer you are trying to get a job with.

3. **Develop a strategy:** The roadmap that takes you from where you are now (SWOT) to where you want to be at some point in the future (SMART objectives).

4. **Define your tactics:** The specific decisions you make and tasks that you undertake along this journey (roadmap) that will take you from where you are to where you want to be at some point in the future. The chapters that follow this one will outline and assist you with these tactical decisions.

5. **Constantly evaluate:** Both along the way, and especially as you reach your objective(s), you should be constantly evaluating and considering alternative routes. Remaining flexible as threats emerge or new opportunities arise is always an important tool in trying to reach your objectives.

6. **Begin again:** Reevaluating means to evaluate *again*, which means the process begins again (or it never really ends). You are a dynamic

being, constantly changing and evolving, as are the Opportunities and Threats that you have no control over. So "SWOT Yourself" with each new job opportunity and begin again ... and again ... and again, as demonstrated in the steps above.

The point is, you need to move. Move yourself in your own direction toward your own dreams. What you choose to do affects your life in the future. If you can move in one direction you can also move in another direction or even in the opposite direction, if needed. Many people put their own needs way down on the list after fulfilling everyone else's needs first, but in your life, you need to move yourself up and start listening to your own needs as well.

Reflecting on your own success stories

Collecting your own success stories along the way will help keep you motivated. Start thinking about yourself in terms of success and ask yourself, *"What are my success stories so far?"* We all have them, both in the tiny moments and the grand achievements of life. These stories can emerge from Professional You or from Personal You. In any job search process you need to give examples of how you have succeeded in the past, using your knowledge, skills and personality. And once you have that job you dreamed of, you will often go through annual performance reviews and possibly salary revisions, where it is very important that you are able to quantify what you bring to the table in terms of helping the company reach its goals. How have you used your skills? What was the outcome of using them? Add the words *Aspirations* and *Results* to your SWOT and write down what you have aspired to and the results you have been getting so far. Make a map of your life leading up to this point and list *all* of your achievements and results so far. Seeing them on paper just might surprise you.

You have already come such a long way; you have already broken down so many obstacles that once seemed impossible to overcome. With that in mind, what you want for the future can't really be that hard to attain, can it? Try to look further than you even think is possible. And then aim even higher than that. Remember though, that hard work will have to follow and nothing truly worthwhile came easily.

Let's look at a couple of examples to help clarify this train of thought. The first story involves someone who had to re-think the objectives he had and learn to prioritize. The second example is about someone who took what she gained in setting and focusing on goals in one area, and using this focus in another:

> **Bjorn** was struggling with a full-time job and working part-time in the family business at the same time. He had two dogs that needed exercise every day and Bjorn was at that point in life where he was considering starting a family in the near future with his wife. Doing it all and wanting to strive for so much at once was counter-productive and Bjorn felt the need to prioritize and cut back on something. He revisited his objectives and thought long and hard about what was really important in his life just then and in the long run. Selling the family business was the way to gain more spare time and the room for building a family. Put another way, giving up one objective made another one more possible for Bjorn.

> Being a professional athlete, **Clara** was used to setting high objectives for herself and she trained hard to reach her goals. Getting back on her feet after failing in an important competition often meant immediately setting new goals for herself and finding a way to motivate herself to reach them. Clara used this focus she learned as an athlete and transferred that mindset into building a successful business that she now runs with several full-time employees. Still constantly having setbacks and from time to time struggling to keep cash flow moving in a positive direction, she realized that the ups and downs are constant and that flexibility, a positive mindset and hard work are the only way to go. She has high standards and is aiming for the stars, and it is paying off.

Find your mentor(s)

It is very rare to go straight from graduating from school (high school; university) to you target or dream job. But you also don't want to set your goals too low. So use LinkedIn (more on this in Chapter 9, *Managing Digital Brand YOU*) to look at other people's positions between graduation and their current position at your target job. If they could get there so can you! And you can copy their transition to get to the same place. Probably they first started at some sort of entry level position within the industry and then gradually moved their way up or they held the desired position but in a different industry before making a horizontal move to where they are now.

A mentor could give you advice and be your role model. You might be pleasantly surprised how easy it is just to show interest in a person and ask them to mentor you. It's amazing how seldom a genuine question like that will be turned down. An example of this is illustrated in the story below involving **Natalie**:

> Natalie wasn't new at her job but felt like she was breaking new ground and in need of advice from someone on a more senior level. She wanted it to be a woman working in the male-dominated industry she found herself working in, and she wanted it to be someone who knew about her challenges but who was not directly involved in her operations. She spent some time trying to identify who she wanted as a mentor and who would fit what she was looking for.
>
> All of a sudden one of the people she had thought of booked a meeting with her, a person from upper-level management by the name of Kris. They had never met before but Natalie had heard of and admired Kris's work. Through this first meeting, which went well, Natalie began to feel comfortable with being able to ask Kris if she wanted to be her mentor.
>
> She explained why she had thought of her as a mentor and what she wanted the mentorship to be like. Kris immediately agreed to be her mentor, as she saw it more as a part of her job then something she should just be willing to do.
>
> As a mentor, Kris really helped push Natalie's career forward. She gave Natalie the courage to let senior management know what her career objectives were and that she was ready to take on new responsibilities. Natalie had needed someone to just listen and give some advice. Not only did she do this, but Kris really followed up and helped to push Natalie's objectives even further than she had ever dreamed of. Her career really jumped from there with just some small tweaks in Natalie's behavior and by just speaking up more about her thoughts and not feeling intimidated in front of senior management, her career began to flourish.

Include a career objective

Often, at the top of your CV, you will have a career goal, which is a simple statement that allows you to use some power words and then adapt what you will deliver to the potential job opportunity you are applying for. Put simply, your career objective, whether in writing or simply stated in an interview, should be like a chameleon: It should change its skin (i.e. wording) to fit the job you are going after. The wording you have in your career objective should focus on what they are looking for in the job ad, not what *you* want out of the job.

Here are two examples of career objectives that are written in different ways. The first one focuses on what the person applying wants to get out of it; the second one lifts what the employer is seeking and announces, *"I am the person you are looking for"* and adds a few power words to hit that point home.

POOR CAREER OBJECTIVE: To get a job that allows me to develop myself as a teacher and make a good living so I can support my family.

Again, in this first example, the person seeking the job is writing down what *they* want to get out of it. A university is not hiring teachers so they can develop themselves – they expect someone who is being hired to teach to have already developed that skill.

So let's rewrite the career objective, only this time lift in what the job ad is seeking:

GOOD CAREER OBJECTIVE: To use my international education and global experience to obtain a position at the assistant/associate professor level at an academic institution within the United States or Sweden.

In this stronger example, the job ad focused on the desire to hire someone at the assistant/associate professor level with a teaching and research focus in international business. So the person writing this at the top of their CV used power words like international and education; then global and experience, to make themselves more connected to what the employer is seeking. The person writing this career objective at the top of their CV also knew that in the job ad they were seeking someone at the assistant/associate professor level to teach and do research in international business, so they delivered themselves as the person who was at this level they were seeking. They simply tailored their career objective to what the employer is seeking.

From career to life objectives

This book is definitely about how to brand and market yourself so as to become a stronger, more attractive candidate for those job openings that you feel you are both qualified for and interested in. However, having a career objective is not enough. The life you will lead (or that you want to lead) will often be dictated by the career path you choose.

What kind of job do you want to have? What kind of organization do you want to work for? What is more important for you in terms of the job and what it requires? Is it the money you make? Is it the flexibility within the job? Is it possibly the fact that the job will pay you to travel? What you need to think about BEFORE you think about your career is your life, as these two elements are not mutually exclusive.

Today, more than ever, they are intertwined and connected in a 24/7 dance that takes a lot of energy to coordinate. Many call this a work/life balance. What we mean is, the career (and jobs within it) that you choose will dictate the life you lead. And the life you lead will greatly influence the type of jobs you go after and the career you develop.

Therefore, before you get started on a career objective and worrying about your CV, let alone any potential interviews that such a document could lead to, it is time to do something simple yet difficult all at the same time: *Think about your life*. If there is anything we have learned, it is that life seems to go by in the snap of a finger. And the older we get, the faster it seems to go by. To assist you with this, we want you to think about some things you want to try, experience, or see before you die.

Many have seen the Warner Bros. movie "The Bucket List" starring Morgan Freeman and Jack Nicholson. In the movie, two men with cancer meet each other in a hospital as they receive treatment. Together they create a Bucket List of things they want to do before they die. "*What do YOU want to do before YOU die?*" For our purposes, we call it a "Life List."

Your list can of course contain whatever you want. It can include some career items. But mostly it should contain life experiences. It can be from the smallest of things (catch a snowflake on your tongue; fall backwards into the snow and make a snow angel) to the grandest of ideas (visit the moon; travel into outer space).

The more specific you can be, the better. Don't just write, "Own a sports car" – but write out what kind (make and model) of sports car and the year (if it's not a new one you want). What color would you like it to be (exterior and interior)? Don't just write, "Travel." Instead, list specific things you want to do or experience at any spot on the globe: See the sunset over the pyramids in Egypt; enjoy sunrise on the Great Wall of China; swim with dolphins in Hawaii; see a buffalo in Yellowstone National Park; spend the night at the Ice Hotel in northern Sweden; see the Grand Canyon in Arizona; make a 3-course meal for my friends and impress them with my cooking; see a Broadway show; visit Central Park in October; see Mount Everest up close; walk along the Appalachian Trail.

Why is this included in a book about Brand YOU? Because Brand YOU is, in the end, a human being with only a finite time left on this earth. Your career will influence the life you lead and what you do in your spare time, just as the life you want to lead will affect your career choices. We use this as an invitation to now visit the exercises that will end this chapter, one of which will be coming up with 100 things you want to do before you die, but make the list even longer if you want to – after all, it's your life!

Workbook – Chapter 5

While Chapter 3 (Getting to Know Brand YOU) and Chapter 4 (Matching Your Brand to the Demands of the Employer) helped you understand the current situation facing Brand YOU, or where you are now, this chapter has focused on helping you understand how to set some specific, measurable objectives for your personal brand, or answer the question of where you want to be at some point in the future. Below are some exercises that will aid you in taking the first step in setting these objectives for yourself.

EXERCISE 5 A – Some basic questions about your future:

- Where do you want to live? Country? Region of that country? City within that region? Large city or small town?

- What type of commute do you want to take to work? How do you want to get to work each day? Drive yourself? Public transportation (subway; bus; taxi)? Walk or ride a bike?

- How many years do you see yourself staying at one workplace and why? NOTE: This is a common question in a job interview.

- What level of responsibility do you think you are ready for? What level are you willing to take on?

- What are your ideal working hours?

- What are your ideal working conditions?

- How do you want to be rewarded for your work?

    - MONTHLY (or hourly) SALARY: _____

    - BENEFITS (circle those that interest you the most)

    - Insurance coverage (medical/dental/life)

    - Company car

    - Cell phone

    - Flexible hours

- Paid vacation

- Gym membership

- Profit sharing

- Ownership/Partnership in the company

- Household services

- Other: _____

EXERCISE 5 B – Make some plans

- **Write your 2-year Plan:** Think two years ahead. What do you want your life to be like? What do you want in your life when it comes to your career? What do you want your salary to be?

- **Write your 5-year Vision:** Think five years ahead. What do you want your life to be like? What do you want in your life when it comes to your career? What do you want your salary to be?

- To help you for both your 2-year and 5-year plans, use the table below to reflect on these types of issues for Brand YOU:

Career	
Relationship(s)	
Health/exercise	
Travel/experiences	
Housing	
Economy	
Interests	

EXERCISE 5 C – Create different career paths

You should always be open to many different career paths and job options, or even the opportunity of running your own company or freelancing/consulting. Thinking on a broader scale about your career will create more opportunities and paths to choose from.

List at least three different career paths or possible first jobs for you after graduation or for you right now at this point in your life?

- Use www.linkedin.com/college/alumni for inspiration from other people's career paths.
- Use the table below to organize in your workbook/journal for this book how to present and discuss three different career paths for yourself, based on your education and experience:

Title & company/ organization you would like to work for:	What are the positive effects of this path?	What are the negative effects/ challenges?	Describe things 5 years in the future at this place:
1.			
2.			
3.			

EXERCISE 5 D – Practice writing a career objective (to go at the top of your CV)

- Start by looking for an actual job opening you think you might like to apply for, either now or at some point in the near future.

- Practice writing a career objective that sounds like that is what you will deliver, but is actually focused on repeating what they are looking for.

- Start your career objective (keep it to one sentence long), often placed at the top of your CV, with the following (you fill in the blank):
  *To use my education and experience to*_____
  _____
  _____.

- Now compare what you wrote? Does it MATCH or somehow connect to what they are looking for (what they are describing) in the job advertisement?

EXERCISE 5 E – Create your own Life List

Take out a piece of paper, or on your computer, start YOUR list right now. Yes, you can have some things on your list that you have already completed, as there is always a sense of accomplishment in checking things off your list. It's up to you, but we suggest no more than 40% of your list should be things you can check off. At least 60% should be kept for things you still have left to do.

And yes, you can take things you no longer want to do off your list and add things anytime you want. You can have 250 things on your list if you want – but start with, and challenge yourself to come up with, 100 as a starting point.

HINT: Let's say you have tried snorkeling, so go ahead, put it on your list and check it off. But let's say you enjoyed that experience. So now you could add something new but related, such as scuba diving. Or if you have gone downhill (slalom) skiing, you may want to try snowboarding. For now, write down your first 10 in the spaces below:

1. _____

2. _____

3. _____

4. _____

5. _____

6. _____

7. _____

8. _____

9. _____

10. _____

CHAPTER 6

Networking Brand YOU

"Succeeding in business is all about making connections."

RICHARD BRANSON

The importance of who you know

The social phenomenon known as "Six Degrees of Kevin Bacon" (yes, the actor) focuses on one main point: You are never more than six people away from meeting anyone else on the planet. There is always someone you know, who knows someone else, who knows someone else, etc., etc.

This "Six degrees" (i.e. six people) that separate us from anyone else is a powerful idea. It means that our network of people, of the people who we know, becomes greatly expanded once we realize it's not just about who we know, but also about who they know, then who those people know, and onward our network grows. An example of this involves connecting a normal, hard-working guy in the middle of his career, working for a corporation in the USA, to the President of the United States (POTUS).

Greg works as a marketing manager for a company that makes tennis racquets. In addition to marketing and selling these racquets around the world, part of his job is seeing to it that his company's brand of tennis racquets ends up in the hands of some of the best professional tennis players who end up on TV in major tournaments around the world.

One of the players that Greg's company used to have a sponsorship deal with is now retired, but this player transcends tennis and is still active with his foundation and he is still famous and a household name. The company Greg works at maintains a working relationship with this retired tennis player for the simple fact that they can continue to be involved with him, primarily to support his foundation.

This player could have his agent pick up the phone and contact the White House Chief of Staff or someone dealing with PR for the White House and ask for a short sit down meeting with the President to discuss his foundation and the need for finding a way to reach out to even more inner-city youth in America to stay active and stay in school. The famous tennis player is then invited to the White House to discuss how to do just that. He knows that "paying" for this is better done through donations and corporate sponsorship, so this tennis player brings Greg along as an example of a partnership in this initiative to take this foundation to work with the White House and move this out to a broader spectrum of youth across the United States.

So how many people did it take to connect Greg to the President of the United States? From Greg, it took only three additional people to connect Greg to sitting down over a cup of coffee with the President:

Greg – Famous Tennis Player – Agent – White House contact – POTUS

Let's use another example, this time using just a normal, everyday high school student by the name of **Hannah**.

Hannah loves food and has a fairly sophisticated palate for a 14-year-old. Her goal is to be accepted into one of the top culinary schools in the world after high school. Her ultimate dream is to become a chef and earn a Michelin Star for her culinary skills. She would love to meet chef Gordon Ramsay.

While Hannah is in only her first year of high school in the Western United States, she knows she could get her parents to drive her to one of Chef Ramsay's more famous restaurants, "Hell's Kitchen" in Los Angeles. However, she wants to meet him, not just see him from a distance or sit down and eat his food.

Hannah has an uncle who lives in Europe. This uncle travels a lot and knows a lot of people So she called him and asked him if he knew anyone who might know someone who might know someone who might know Gordon Ramsay. One of her uncle's good friends was a chef who had opened many successful restaurants in Scandinavia, even though he was originally from London. This uncle then asked his friend, who said he did know someone who had studied under Ramsay and in fact worked in one of Chef Ramsay's restaurants back home in London. As with Greg meeting POTUS, Hannah was only three people away from meeting Chef Gordon Ramsay:

Hannah – Uncle – Friend of uncle – Chef in London – Chef Ramsay

Of course, there are no guarantees that such networks will end up with you actually meeting someone. The fictional examples above only illustrate the idea that it's not really about who you know, but about how your network is a series of other networks that can provide you with a myriad of opportunities.

As discussed earlier in the book, your reputation (image) will follow you wherever you go. A lot of job opportunities are filled before they are even advertised, as the employer or recruiting firm knows who they want and are often just following formal rules of hiring for any type of job opportunity that needs to be filled. Other times, it's a matter of knowing who they do *not* want, so your name and reputation can open opportunities or close up these opportunities just as quickly, depending on who you know and what they know (or think) about you.

There are many common uses for the 80/20 rule, also known as the Pareto Principle. In fact, it is used so often and in so many situations, it is almost cliché. But something becomes a cliché over time, probably due to it being true time and again. For this chapter, the following 80/20 rule should be taken seriously:

> "Your success is 20% what you know, 80% who you know."

There is no source for this quote, but it is a generally-accepted idea about the power that your network plays in terms of your success. It is highlighted here to get you thinking about the idea that so much of your success will be based on a combination of two things: Your education and experience (i.e. WHAT you know), but also your network – and the networks of those people in your network, as we just demonstrated with the examples in "Six Degrees of Kevin Bacon" – (i.e. WHO you know). This focus on what, but especially who, you know, combined with the people and communication skills needed when contacting and interacting with these people, will ultimately play more of a role in your career successes(es) than you can possibly imagine.

As was stated above, many jobs are never even advertised. Instead they are offered directly within a network or through recommendations. For other jobs, some of the employers might already have someone in mind who they want to hire but want to advertise the position just to market the fact that the company is expanding or hiring for these types of jobs.

Other times it is required by law that a position within an organization be publicly available (communicated), whether someone is already in mind for the job or not.

Often, people will recommend people they know for certain jobs. If they don't know you, how could they recommend you? But it is not enough that they know you. They need to know your positive traits. The idea here is that you need to find and constantly update a strong list of people who will act as a reference. Some of them write reference letters. Others call it a letter of recommendation. Either way, you need these people in your corner before you even think about working on your CV.

But what makes someone a "good" reference for you? Who should be someone you ask for a letter of recommendation? Every person who you ask to write a letter or act as a reference for you needs to fulfill five very important criteria:

- They know about you professionally
- They know about you personally (your personality)
- They can describe you in positive ways (i.e. what are your strengths?)
- They can describe you in negative ways (i.e. what are your weaknesses?) – and they can do so without messing up the job for you
- They are strong communicators: They can write a good reference letter; they are good on the phone with others.

Now think about it a minute … how many people, who are not family or close friends, can meet those five criteria above? So your network can help you connect to others, it can open up job opportunities for you, but it is also what provides you with references. What all of the above have in common is that it all comes down to you and your reputation, where how others see you (your image) is your most valuable asset.

Image really *is* everything

Remember in Chapter 1 when we discussed IDENTITY vs. IMAGE? Then in Chapter 3 we asked you to compare your Identity (what you think of yourself; how you want to be perceived) with your Image (what others actually think of you). When we speak of "reputation" we are speaking of your image, or what others think of you. As a brand, you need to stand out and be memorable, albeit in a positive way. Your reputation is something you earn, but it is also something you can learn to influence and manage as well.

It starts day one of your first job. And if you're already working, it should be noted that people in your organization or industry already associate you with different adjectives, or ways of describing you in both positive and negative terms. Nearly everything you say and do can affect your professional reputation, both positively and negatively. What would your references say about you? And how about those that are *not* one of your references? Imagine that your coworkers are talking about you. What would they say? How do you come across to other people?

Now imagine that your managers or bosses are doing the same. What would they talk about? Would they speak about you positively or negatively? Would you be described as a positive or negative team member? Are you a high or low performer? What if you are currently the boss? If you have employees you are managing, what would they say? Everything that is being said about you becomes the truth within your network. Good and bad. And if you are not aware of it you can't do anything about it (i.e. try and manage or influence it).

Now, think about what you can do, starting today, to enhance your reputation. Is there something you need to change? Being good at what you do is step 1 to building a really good professional reputation. Everything else you do should be seen as a way to enhance it.

The size of the circles in Figure 6.1 below is no coincidence. While all of these elements are important, it is the WHO you know (and HOW they know you) that outshine WHAT you know (that combination of education plus experience that takes up nearly all of your CV).

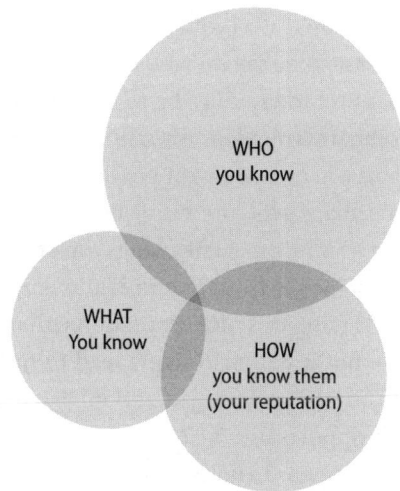

WHO you know

WHAT You know

HOW you know them (your reputation)

FIGURE 6.1
The career trilogy of WHAT, WHO & HOW.

Working in a larger organization, the words (or lack of ones) about you will either enhance your performance or put traps before you as this example will illustrate:

> **Melina** was working as a project manager within a company with 1500+ employees. Her line of work involved coordinating bigger company events and being a representative to clients and partners in other organizations. Being a positive, people person she was always making sure to say hi and make small talk to everyone within the company as she met them during the day, no matter if it was someone in senior management or the staff working at the company cafeteria.
>
> Although unaware of it herself, this positive behavior made her work performance more efficient. When she needed something done fast, before an event deadline, she could call upon the cleaning staff for extra cleaning or she could easily get senior management to approve things faster. Everyone, whether higher up, on the same level or below her in the company hierarchy would prioritize her requests simply because she had a nice personality – she was nice to them! She talked to them and knew their names. Melina's greatest strength, in fact, was that she treated everyone, regardless of position or rank, with kindness and respect.

People like to help nice people. They are not nearly as likely to help not-so-nice people. Everyone, no matter their position, is powerful enough to have at least some say on whose request they will prioritize; what work they will focus on today. Having a broad network and a nice reputation within the company you work for will help you achieve your results faster and better than you even thought possible. Reputation (image) is that important. And this image gets communicated not only within the organization, but outside of it as well, especially when you are seeking a new opportunity and need to use someone from that previous employer as a "reference."

Having this nice reputation will not only help you achieve more on your job, but it will also likely lead to more job (advancement) opportunities within the same organization, or even job offers from other organizations. Job opportunities are given through contacts and contacts are given by working hard and being nice. So the "golden rules" are simple for us all:

1. Work hard.
2. Be nice.

Or, put simply, *"Work Nice!"*

Yes, it's common sense. But we have all been around more than enough people who were not nice or nice to work with. The people who know you as hard working and nice are more likely to hire you rather than trying someone who they don't know, no matter if their experience outshines yours. The people who know you will recommend you to others and pass your good reputation on. An example of this involves two fictional colleagues who had worked together for years:

> **Leonel** moved to a new town and started to work at a big organization without knowing anyone there. Little did he know that in a few years he would have changed his job description and title several times, expanded his network and be in the position where he had the opportunity to start a whole new department. When this happened, he called upon Erika, with whom he had been working when he first started his career. He knew that if he could get her on board, then the department would become really successful. Erika was not hard to convince, as she knew Leonel was a hard worker and she enjoyed working with him. However, she also knew that she would have never accepted if she didn't already know about his personality and how it was to work with him.

How do you gain a better understanding of your reputation (image)? You do it by getting feedback from managers, colleagues, business partners and employees, as well as from customers. This is known as 360 Degree Feedback, and it is a tool that you can use in order to start seeing yourself as others see you. And what if you do hear negative things? See those as an invitation to better understand your weaknesses and allow you to focus on what you can work on to improve yourself. And what about the positive things? See those as an invitation to do more of the same. Here is another example to illustrate this:

> Almost seven years after leaving her former employer **Miranda** received a call from the owner of the company with a new job offer. Miranda was surprised by this, as it came right out of the blue since they had not had much contact over the few years since she had left for another job opportunity.
>
> The offer was both generous and flexible. Her former employer was starting a new business and wanted to hire people he knew to be reliable, hard working with a passion for what they did. It was more important to him to find the right people than people with the "proper" education or "perfect" qualifications. He had known Miranda as extremely driven, and positive and he knew that she would always go the extra mile and create good results for the company.

If you are genuinely interested, then be sure and show that to people in your field. If you are not genuinely interested, then perhaps it is time to start looking into a different field or another job opportunity. If you're not genuine, people will notice and avoid you. Ask questions instead of just talking about yourself. Others will be interested in you if you show interest in them. Remember faces, names and the companies or departments they work for. And make sure your brand is memorable enough for them to also remember you. Make sure to use social media such as LinkedIn to keep your network and references in one easy access place so you don't risk losing track of them. This is what happened to someone in the next example:

> **Tom** was being interviewed for a different position within the company for which he had been working for over 5 years. He had a good reputation and a lot of references within the company. However, now they were asking him for references outside of the company. Luckily he still had a good relationship with his former employers and called them to let them know which position he was applying for and asked them to be his references again. Because of how Tom had been when he worked there, and because his relationship with them ended on a positive note, they were most happy to remain a strong reference for him. He also made sure to refresh their memory about his greatest accomplishments and the results and achievements he wanted them to emphasize. Of course he landed the new job.

Another part of great networking is turning your "enemies" to "frienemies." This means keeping and maintaining as good relationships as possible with others, even with the people that you do not particularly like or that might not like you. This way they are less likely to stab you in the back or say anything negative. So make sure you do not forget to stay in contact and treat those people with kindness as well. Keeping your enemies close will decrease the chance for them to harm you in a professional setting. Here is an example of this:

> Being understaffed for a long time, **Joline** was managing her department with a very tight list of priorities. This meant she cancelled meetings that she thought were just politics and there to maintain relationships with other managers, and she was just completely focused on the task at hand. She realized too late that this meant that someone whom she needed to be onboard with her decisions was working with an agenda that would collide with her own. If she would have maintained communication with the person she would have had an easier time completing her tasks. Now she spent three weeks trying to sort out a major conflict that was completely unnecessary, as this person she needed felt ignored and did not prioritize Joline when Joline most needed him.

Making time for communicating with others and cultivating relationships does not have to mean three-hour meetings. Sometimes it means just staying in touch, helping out when you can, especially those that are difficult to work with – simply put, *make people feel understood and appreciated!* Ask for their opinion whenever possible. Involve them in what you are doing, even though you may struggle to get along with some of them. It will make your professional life so much easier and it is time well spent, because it will be time invested in relationships that make up your network. And your network is filled with people you like/don't like and who like/don't like you in return.

Finding mentors within your organization and outside of it will not only be helpful for career advice but a mentor can also push you out of your comfort zone and introduce you to new people and help you expand your network and spread the word. This can help you during times you seek a promotion or different kind of assignment within the organization, as this example demonstrates:

Lisa was the first person in her family to graduate from university, so she felt she had no one to turn to for advice on crossing that bridge from university education to starting a career using her newly-minted degree. At school she had not received any coaching or career advice, such as salary negotiation or in making difficult career decisions. Once she was hired after graduation, Lisa felt the need to talk to someone in upper-level management for advice. So she cultivated relationships within the organization she was working for and started to discuss these things with one person in particular who had followed a similar path. She never asked them to be a mentor for her, but deep down that is was what she thought they were doing anyway. Lisa simply, and informally, developed relationships with people she knew she could turn to for advice and help when she needed it.

Growing your network

Take the initiative and start to connect with and contact people. Start going out to lunch with different people. Let them know that you are looking for career advice. Initiative, however, does not mean going around handing your business card out like it was a deck of cards, pushing it on to people when mingling. Yes, this happens and no, it will not usually do you any good. And other than within your own organization, where else can you develop professional relationships with people who could advise you and answer your questions?

Going to conferences, courses and workshops within your field will not only add to your knowledge base but also grow your network and from that your reputation. Sharing your knowledge by offering to speak at a conference or holding a workshop is a good way to build your brand and become more known within your field. Business events and mingles are more important to your career than you imagine, as that is where important people meet and career decisions are often made, or at least influenced. It is at these events that you need to be seen and to use such opportunities as a way to connect to people and grow your network.

Of course, there are plenty of pitfalls to be aware of in networking. The obvious pitfall is networking just to get something from others, which is a form of simply trying to use people. *"Givers gain"* is a common statement within networking. It's not just about you meeting others, but letting others meet you! You should be generous with your networking and your knowledge. If you give, you are more likely to receive. Your interest in other people needs to be genuine and you need to focus on building lasting, meaningful relationships instead of just "connections" that you can use.

Approaching people with a genuine interest in what they do, with no hidden agenda, is the best way to build those relationships. Whether or not such encounters might evolve into doing business together in the future should not be the focal point in the beginning. It's about using and practicing your people and communication skills on a regular basis. Walking into a situation filled with only a room filled with strangers is a fear many people have. But pushing yourself outside your comfort zone is where the magic happens. Meeting only with people you already know won't grow your network – it only maintains the one you already have.

Sometimes you hear people make comments like: *"Well, he can't do anything for me, so why should I help him?"* Not only is that a pessimistic way to look at people, but you also have no idea who will be important for your career in the future. Sometimes people come on too strong, too pushy, or are simply too aggressive. Take the time to at least start a conversation with them. This is the art of true networking. Cultivating good relationships just for the benefit of being a nice person will always be the best way to live your life, be it for professional or personal reasons.

Another pitfall is failing to understand that every job you ever have is important to your professional reputation and that you need to do your very best in order to get good recommendations and references from everywhere you work and everyone you work with. Do your best to try and end every job on a positive note. This won't always work out, but no matter what, ask for a final conversation or what is known as an exit interview. Get feedback, and perhaps a recommendation, from your manager at that time. Either way, always try and end things with a handshake and a smile.

Your future employers will take references even from people you have not listed as your references. They will call other people you have worked for; they will ask colleagues, partners or customers; sometimes they don't even have to do the calling themselves, as your former boss might actually call them up, either to congratulate them on a good hire (or possibly to warn them). It's a small world more often than not, and in a specific field of business or within a particular industry, it gets even smaller. So it is important to realize that people in these small worlds know each other ...

and yes, they talk. Remember, there is always someone who knows someone who knows someone else.

However, managing your reputation means you should always be yourself. It's just that, especially for Professional You, and even Personal You, you should always try and be the best, most positive person you can be. It sounds like a cliché, and in many ways it is. But your reputation starts with how you project yourself. It ends (positively or negatively) with how others see you (again, your image).

As will be discussed more in Chapter 9, *Managing Digital Brand YOU*, it is important to note here that you should understand that social media, if used wisely, can definitely enhance or add to your reputation in a positive way. However, if used unwisely, it can do the exact opposite, affecting your professional reputation in a negative way. And people do use social media without thinking what it does to their professional reputation.

There are real-life examples of people losing their jobs due to being part of a dubious Facebook group, having a questionable picture posted with them in it, or writing something inappropriate about their job or employer on social media. Please be aware that it can affect your personal brand if you write that you don't like your job, if you constantly have pictures of yourself drinking alcohol, or if you express too many political opinions that might irritate people.

It's one thing to express your personal opinions on a variety of subjects. It's another thing to do it constantly or take such opinions too far. And remember, how you *intend* something to be taken isn't always the way it is taken by someone else.

TIP: Reflect before you open your mouth and say anything, before you write a letter, e-mail or post-it note to be given to someone else, or post to or comment on anything coming up in any of the social media you are involved in:

- Does what you are writing or posting really need to be said?
- Does it need to be said *now*?
- Is this *really* the right place/forum to say it?
- Are you saying/writing it to the right people?

Remember, not everyone feels as strongly as you about certain issues and they could easily get the wrong picture of you if you express yourself too strongly. In a democracy, everyone has the right to say and express themselves in almost any way they choose. But having that right does not mean you need to take it so far that it ends up hurting your chances for a new job or advancement within the organization you are currently with.

You might have heard the phrase: *"When you need your network, it's too late to build it!"* In fact, you always need good relationships and an extended network. But the good news is that it's never too late to start building it. So from now on, show interest in other people. Broaden your horizons, be genuinely nice. Give and you shall receive.

Summary and helpful tips to expand your network:

- Get a mentor
- Go to conferences, courses and workshops
- Share your knowledge
- Go to business events and social mingles
- Take the initiative and contact people
- Be your most positive self
- Be good at what you do
- Show genuine interest in other people
- Befriend your enemies ("Kill" them with kindness)
- Work hard; be nice (or *"Work nice!"*)

Even though you now have the best self-awareness, objectives for the future and a good understanding of the importance of a network you still need a way to get you from where you are now to a point you want to be in the future. This roadmap that takes you from where you are now towards your career and life objectives is called a strategy. For our purposes, we will focus this strategy on a series of tactical decisions that relate to communicating Brand YOU, which will be the focus of Chapters 7–9. However, before you start with that, don't forget to do the exercises for Chapter 6.

Workbook – Chapter 6

This chapter has focused on Networking Brand YOU. Below, you will find a few questions to think about and write down in whatever format you are using to take part in these exercises. Remember, success is based 20% on what you know, but 80% on who you know!

EXERCISE 6 A – Who are your best references at this point in time?

Remember the five criteria of what makes a good reference:

- They know about you professionally
- They know about you personally (your personality)
- They can describe you in positive ways (i.e. what are your strengths)?
- They can describe you in negative ways (i.e. what are your weaknesses – and they can do so without messing up the job for you)
- They are strong communicators: They can write a good reference letter; they are good on the phone

Based on this, write down the names of three viable references you could use (remember this can change for each job opportunity you go after). For now, start a list of good references for Brand YOU:

NAME: _____

NAME: _____

NAME: _____

EXERCISE 6 B – Your Private vs. Personal vs. Professional Networks

These can include people you know, who in turn know people. For example, you have someone in your personal network (a friend or family member) who you know has contact with another person, who likely has contact with someone else. So everyone you know counts, and your networks never end, they are limitless in all directions. But not everyone in your network is a Reference or should write a letter of recommendation. Name at least three people in each of the following categories who are strong parts of your various networks:

Private network	Personal network	Professional network

EXERCISE 6 C – Establishing new networks

Go to a business network and talk to at least 5 people you did not know before. Ask about their company and what they do there and what they like most about their job and what the challenges are. Exchange business cards. Write their names and what they work with here along with the positive and the challenges:

Name	Company and title	Positive	Challenges
1.			
2.			
3.			
4.			
5.			

EXERCISE 6 D – Conduct a "Six Degrees of Kevin Bacon" experiment

- Write down the name of a famous person (preferably someone a bit more positive in the eyes of the media). Perhaps a President (present or past but still alive); perhaps an actor, musician or author that you're a fan of.

- Then start with the FIRST person that you know personally, who would start you on a path towards meeting with that famous person.

- Then ask that person who they might know who could take you one step further to meeting the famous person you listed.

- The idea is that you won't need more than six people to get to that chance to meet that person whose name you just wrote down.

- If it helps, build your network forward toward that person; then perhaps build a network backwards from the person you are trying to meet.

CHAPTER 7

Communicating Brand YOU in writing

"Emphasize your strengths on your résumé, in your cover letters and in your interviews. It may sound obvious, but you'd be surprised how many people simply list everything they've ever done. Convey your passion and link your strengths to measurable results. Employers and interviewers love concrete data."

MARCUS BUCKINGHAM

While networking is important in order for you to get a foot in the door and to get yourself on the employer's or recruiter's radar, you still need a good cover letter and CV to provide within your network. So knowing people is not enough. You also need to present yourself strongly on paper (real or digital), which is what this chapter is about. Then use these documents as invitations to be invited to an interview, which is what communicating Brand YOU in person (Chapter 8) and on social media (Chapter 9) is all about.

Technology is changing the way you communicate your brand in writing. However, the use of social media, websites, and online CV forums such as LinkedIn.com will be discussed in Chapter 9. For now the focus will be on some of the more traditional, paper-based methods that are still being used in many industries and by many companies and organizations today. More specifically, this chapter will focus on how to develop a cover letter and CV (curriculum vitae), or, as some refer to it, resume or résumé.

The trend in the 21st century is increasingly that we create these documents on our computer or smart device, then turn them into PDF files or Word documents that are then uploaded or attached to an email. However, many organizations continue to ask you to mail in paper versions of such documents as well. Either way, you will never be more "perfect" than you are in your cover letter and CV – so each of these documents in and of themselves need to be perfect as well.

In marketing, we often refer to the theory called hierarchy of effects, of which the most common is called A-I-D-A. It refers to the series of effects that you want someone to pass through, a series of stages that are also the marketing objectives that are developed for brands all over the world. It stands for Awareness (or sometimes Attention); Interest; Desire; Action.[1] For our purposes, since you are now the brand, we feel you must pass through each of these stages as well, which is what we will help you prepare for in this chapter and the next chapter. Below is an example of how this works for most people seeking a job in a competitive market:

Awareness: They have probably not heard of you. So you use your cover letter and CV to create this awareness about Brand YOU.

Interest: Based on your CV, they become interested enough to call you in for a *first* interview.

Desire: Your performance in the first interview went so well they pass you along to a second interview, where three finalists for the job opening are interviewed by someone higher up in the organization.

Action: They offer *you* the job.

Before you send in your cover letter/CV, let alone agree to an interview if you are invited to one after sending in these documents, ask yourself the following questions:

- What does this job include? What is it asking me to do?
- Do I want to work at an organization like this, with these kinds of tasks? If yes, then why? What is my motivation?
- What kinds of skills are needed to do this job? Do my skills match these demands of the employer?
- Would I be happy in this environment? Do I share this organization's values?

---

1 Moriarty, Mitchell and Wells (2009), Advertising: Principles and Practice, London: Pearson Educational International.

Everyone wants to feel special, even the employer

The biggest mistake a job seeker can make is to write a cover letter and a CV and just randomly send it out to every employer or for every job ad that interests them. *Please*, do not let this be you, *ever!* Your cover letter needs to be tailor-made, word-for-word, and your CV will need some updating here and there for each job opportunity and each potential employer you send it out to. Everyone wants to feel special, even the employer. If they feel they are just another "Cc:" on your mailing list, they will not be interested in you, and as in any relationship, the best way to get someone interested in you is by showing interest in them.

So the first step is to give some serious thought to WHAT you want to communicate about yourself, to WHOM and in what CONTEXT? What image do you want to develop? Who is the target here? What are they looking for? What is important to highlight in this specific context? How will you get their attention?

The cover letter should highlight those specific areas of experience and qualifications from your CV that match the specific job you're applying for. It should get the reader interested in reading more about Brand YOU in your CV. The cover letter is not a personal letter; it's a professional letter that needs to be short and to the point, clearly describing why you are interested in that specific job and company and why you are a good match for them. So read the job ad thoroughly and carefully. Read it more than once. Soft/transferable skills described in the job ad are often missed by job-seekers, and a common mistake is to only highlight your educational background and work experience, while failing to describe how your *transferable skills* also match what they are looking for.

It is important to quantify your results instead of just talking about how much you enjoyed the work and how fun or challenging it was. The words you use are very important. Of course the employer wants you to show passion for the work, but passion is best shown in quantified results, positive feedback from others, and references and a solid track record.

Some examples of quantifying your results:

- EXAMPLE 1: I worked as a manager with six people reporting to me and was responsible for an annual budget of $1 million.

- EXAMPLE 2: I sold items worth $100,000 in a week and thereby reached my sales quota for the month three weeks ahead of time.

- EXAMPLE 3: For each event, I attracted up to 2000 visitors and managed a team of 20 volunteers.

Recruiters and people from HR (Human Resources) at organizations read hundreds of applications every single day and they will spend about 15 seconds on yours. Let those 15 seconds matter and focus on WHY you want to work for them and WHAT you can do for them and HOW you have demonstrated this in the past. Doing this in about 3–4 paragraphs is enough. Never start your cover letter with the sentence *"Hi, my name is ... and I am ... years old"*. Your introduction needs to be strong and convince them to keep reading. An example of this comes from a letter from **Valarie** for a potential job opening as a dentist:

> "I am writing in regards to your job opening for a part-time dentist at your dental clinic in East Lansing, Michigan. I understand that the position is part-time as you seek help during peak periods as well as those times when one of the full-time dentists is away or unavailable. I am currently board certified in the State of Michigan. As the rest of this letter and my enclosed CV will show, my education and experience fit this current job opening."

This opening paragraph captures their attention and tells them from the very beginning you are what they are looking for (even though you should never write that). Let them decide that you are qualified or right for the position. A good cover letter leads to them checking out your CV. And your CV becomes the "invitation" to interview you.

Content, structure, layout and language

While the content of your cover letter and CV are key factors in terms of Brand YOU in writing, so is the structure, layout and the language of these written tools you use – and you need to pay them all equal attention.

- **Content:** Focus on *quantifiable* descriptions of your results: What skills do you have? What are you trained/certified in and how this can be useful for them? Make sure the content of your cover letter and CV is rewritten for each job opportunity. As stated earlier, the one-size-fits-all approach should rarely, if ever, be utilized. Instead, it is recommended that your cover letter and CV are adapted specifically to each new job opportunity you are applying for.

- **Audience:** Read the job advertisement, find out as much as you can, then use the wording in your cover letter and CV to more closely align with what they are looking for. So many people end up not being invited to an interview because their CV was simply too vague; too disconnected from what the employer was looking for with regards to that specific job opportunity. Never exaggerate or lie about how well you match, but let what you write demonstrate to them that you are a very good match, based on what they wrote in the job ad.

- **Structure:** Here you should focus on which headings to use and in what order of importance things should be presented for this particular job/employer. Making sure that everything is in reverse chronological order with the *most recent* qualifications (in terms of education, work experience, etc.) listed first helps to tell your story.

- **Layout:** a clear layout with easy to read headings and subheadings using professional font, often Times New Roman (looks good in regular text, *italicized text*, **bold text**, or ***bold italicized text***). Arial is another simple, professional font to use. See the end of the chapter for some simple but effective layout design ideas for you to get started on your CV.

- **Language:** use professional, clear and concise language conveying what you can contribute with – and again, connect the language you use in some careful but clever ways to the language/words they use in their advertising/announcement for that particular job opportunity.

It all begins with a cover letter

Writing a cover letter may seem like an easy task. However, so many people don't bother doing their best work when it comes to writing a cover letter, either because they don't think anyone reads the letter or they think it's really only about the CV. Think again. Even if they only glance over your letter, they are still left with a feeling about it, a feeling that ends up being either positive or negative, professional or unprofessional. And if they are looking for anything, it is about how well you match up with the job opportunity they are offering. Many times, even if they just take a quick look at the cover letter, they will come back to it if your CV makes them interested in interviewing you.

Even if a cover letter is not read word for word, it still leaves an impression on the person who simply, glances at it. While it is suggested that both a cover letter and your CV should be like a chameleon, i.e. you need to change or adapt the wording to adapt to the specific company and job opportunity you are applying for, the following are some general tips and a guideline for how you should put your cover letter together:

- First, create your own letterhead stationery. This is a fairly simple, straightforward task that provides the chance to repeat the brand name (that would be *your* name).
- Letterhead designs that are recommended include:
- Name + contact info at the top of the page
- OR Name at top + contact info at the bottom
- Keep the design simple. Don't use "cute" graphics.
- Make sure that your spacing is correct and that you have 1-inch (2.5 cm) margins on all four sides.
- Check that your spacing between sections is as follows:
- 4 SPACES from the bottom of your name and contact info at the top of the page to the line that has the date the letter is written.

- 4 SPACES from the date to the name and contact info (address, etc.) of the recipient. If no name, then have a headline here that states "Application for job opening xyz".

- 2 SPACES from the last line of the recipient's address to the opening salutation

- 2 SPACES from the opening salutation to the first paragraph

- 2 SPACES from the end of the final paragraph to the closing salutation

- 4 SPACES between the closing salutation and your printed name (to leave space for your signature). If you are uploading or attaching a PDF of your letter to an email, then just two spaces are needed between the closing salutation and your name.

- Set the proofing language to the language you are writing in to help find and correct spelling and grammar mistakes.

- Always proof your letter carefully for spelling, grammar and flow. Flow is how one sentences flows into the next one; and how one paragraph flows into the other.

- Also, have someone else proofread anything in writing before you send it off.

- MOST IMPORTANT: Learn how to K.I.S.S. when writing documents like a cover letter. As important as this letter is in demonstrating your communication skills, remember to **Keep It Short and Simple**.

A sample letter is provided (see Figure 7.1).

John Smith

123 Main Street, 972 55 Luleå • TEL: (321)-123-12345 • E-MAIL: JohnSmith@xyz.com

4 spaces

January 15, 2012

4 spaces

Susan Johnson, CEO
Fun Toys, Inc
123 Toy Drive
971 87 Luleå

2 spaces

Dear Ms. Johansson,

2 spaces

I am writing in regards to the job opening for at marketing director at Fun Toys, Inc, as described at the website toyjobs.com. This should be a short, simple opening, and a short, simple letter.

The you write a paragraph about you *professionally*. Highlight your education and work experience. Be careful not to share too much, as you want the letter to push them to the CV. Remember, the CV is what gets you into a job interview.

Then you write a paragraph about you *personally*. Focus on your strengts as others see you (*"Others often describe me as..."*). Find two to three adjectives, or words that describe you, with a sentence to illustrates each one of them.

Your final paragraph is a closing. To thank the reader and push them to your CV. Write something like, "Thank you for your time and consideratione with this matter. I look forward to hearing from you should my enclosed CV meet your expectations."

2 spaces

Kind Regards,

4 spaces

John Smith

John Smith

FIGURE 7.1 Sample Cover Letter.

Within the letter above are some tips on what to include in the letter, following a simple, four-paragraph system. This is outlined in more detail here:

Following the K.I.S.S. approach (Keep It Short and Simple), it is recommended your *one-page* cover letter focuses on the following four paragraphs (P1, P2, etc.):

1. P1 – INTRODUCTION: Here you want to let the reader know why you are writing and make them want to read the rest of the letter. The intro paragraph is like a lead paragraph in a newspaper or magazine article: It is the "Who, What, Where, When, Why" (or the more important of these elements) that sets up the rest of what the reader will be exposed to. It should make them want to read on.

2. P2 – PROFESSIONAL YOU: Here you want to focus on connecting your *education* and *experience* to what the job description is looking for. Too many letters tend to ramble on about things that have nothing to do with the job description. Here you want to highlight two or three things regarding your education; then two or three things that connect to your experience, as they pertain to the job you are applying for. If education is more important for the job opportunity you are applying for, then start with and focus more on that; if the job seems to focus more on experience within the area they are trying to fill, then start with and focus more on that. This could also be broken up into two shorter paragraphs, as long as it does not make your letter longer than one page.

3. P3 – PERSONAL YOU: This is not a paragraph about your personal life, your personal problems, or your hobbies and interests. They might ask you about those things in an interview, but it is primarily about your *personality*. More specifically, it should focus on lifting out those strengths you have, according to other people. In other words, don't write, *"I consider myself to be ..."* Instead, write, *"Others often describe me as ..."* This implies, of course, that you are actually aware of and being honest about what others think of you. It is important to note that you should not volunteer your weaknesses in a cover letter. Those will certainly be asked about or discovered in the interview(s) you might take part in, just as every reference you

use will be asked the same question: *"Why shouldn't we hire Mary?"* or *"What is wrong with Mike?"*

4. P4 – CLOSING: This is the paragraph that many people seem to make the most mistakes with. There often seems to be this feeling of entitlement for writers of cover letters, where the end often focuses on using statements such as *"I expect to hear from you soon,"* or even the more polite *"I look forward to hearing from you soon".* When you end that way you sound a bit presumptuous – as if you expect to hear from them no matter what. While most organizations are thankful that people apply for their openings, you need to leave it up to them to decide if you are right for the job or to invite you for an interview. So this final paragraph allows you to end on a positive but humble note and make them curious enough to want to read your CV. This could be as simple as 2–3 sentences. SAMPLE CLOSING: *"Thank you for your time and consideration with my application for this opportunity with your organization regarding job opening 'X'* (repeat the name of the job opening – another chance to connect it to you). *I look forward to hearing from you should my enclosed CV meet your expectations."* In other words PUSH them to the CV.

From Letter to CV

A CV (curriculum vitae) can also be known as a resume. Many people wonder why some refer to this document as a CV while others call it a resume (also spelled résumé). While it can vary from industry to industry, according to jobsearch.about.com[2], the primary difference has to do with length. While a resume is usually a 1–2 page summary of your education, experience and skills, a CV often includes the same but then adds additional items, such as a publication list if you work in academia, for example. For our purposes, we use the terms CV and resume interchangeably, implying a 1–2 page summary of your education, experience and skills.

You are never more perfect than you are on your CV, yet there is no such thing as the perfect CV either. A CV is the story about you, your

---

2 For comparison of CV vs. Resume, as well as tips on layout, see http://jobsearch.about.com/cs/curriculumvitae/f/cvresume.htm (ACCESSED: September 15, 2015).

accomplishments so far, your achievements and successes, all presented in a way that will attract your target employer to do one thing: *Invite YOU to an interview!*

Too many people think a CV is what gets them hired. If an employer does this, then they are hiring a piece of paper or a PDF file, not a person. And employers should be in the habit of hiring the right kinds of people, not the perfect pieces of paper! You need to meet the person behind that perfected version that is presented on paper, and you need to meet that potential employer as well. As one hiring manager, let's call her **Chloe,** told us:

"Reading through over 100 applications with a tight deadline on the hiring process, even though nothing else is taken off from my busy schedule, both personally and professionally, makes the reading of CVs and cover letters often a speed read at best. I do this due to my busy schedule, even though I fully understand that the hiring of staff is the major investment for my office this year. But in my mind I think: 'If you don't sell yourself immediately to me, either through your letter or CV (whichever I open first), I will reject you.'

How can you sell our services to stakeholders, partners and customers if you cannot even sell yourself and your skills? I look for matches to the skills we listed in the job ad, but too many applicants miss the opportunity to sell me those skills and end up focusing on other things instead. Why?

I'd rather just take the recommendation from someone I trust than read through a ton of CVs, nearly all of which look so good but I don't know if they actually ARE that good or if they have any motivation whatsoever to do good work for our organization. Interviews can deceive you. It's better to ask within your network for recommendations and headhunt that way. But part of my job is to go through all potential applicants, and so I do. You never know where the ideal candidate will come from.

Working in a big organization, I often get applicants from within the organization as well. People I have met on different occasions. People who could be a perfect fit, but fail to make a good impression just by failing to contact me about the fact that they are interested in working at my department. They just send in an online application, when they could have called, emailed or come by my office beforehand to tell me that they are interested and why. Seeing their applications and not hearing from them personally before I receive their documents makes me think that they are running away from something instead of being genuinely interested in moving towards a new opportunity."

So while a cover letter opens up the communication, it really is used as a precursor to the most important document you will ever develop when it comes to Brand YOU: Your CV.

See your CV as an invitation

Although it happens at times, no one should be hired straight off the back of their CV. There is no such thing as a perfect CV and cover letter. What the truly right candidate has is a strong combination of written application (cover letter and CV), reputation, network and interpersonal skills. None of these factors needs to be perfect in and of themselves. It's the combination of these things working together that makes for a great match between employer and employee. So a cover letter and CV alone will never get you hired. Together they become an invitation to an interview.

The top of your CV (or resume) should say just that, as it tells the reader what the document is. Below this, use the same heading (your name and contact info) that you had on your letterhead stationery. Then organize your CV into precise sections. As a general guideline, these sections should include, but not necessarily be limited to, the following areas (and often, but not always, in this order):

- Education
- Work Experience (i.e. what you have been paid for)
- Additional Experience (i.e. what you have been involved in)
- Additional Skills (e.g. language skills, specific software skills they require; computer language/programming skills; driver's license if they require one; etc.)
- Awards & Honors
- References

Remember to keep dates flush left, as it is easier to keep track that way, and always start with the most recent item first within each section, working back in time as you go down the list. Don't go too far back, as some items within each section become less relevant the more time has passed.

Being awarded MVP (most valuable player) for your high school football team does not really matter once you reach a certain age or start to go after certain kinds of jobs after college.

CV layout

In terms of layout, CVs take on all sorts of different looks. Use Google or even such social media as Pinterest and write "CV layout" or "Layouts for resumes." As with the cover letter, a K.I.S.S. (Keep It Short and Simple) approach is recommended in most cases.

The very first section in a CV can vary. Some people use a Profile as their first section, or a brief "bio" of the subject of the CV. However, we recommend the use of a Career Objective for one simple reason: From the start, it connects Brand YOU to the actual job opportunity. It's a clever way of matching your brand to what they are looking for. As we discussed earlier, an example of this is as follows: *"To use my education and experience to ..."* Then fill in the rest of that sentence to connect to, or actually name specifically, the job opening they are offering.

In terms of your section on Education, stay focused on three areas:

- The type of degree: An associate's, bachelor's (B.A. or B.S.), or master's degree (M.A. or M.S.)? Doctorate (Ph.D.) or professional (e.g. medical or law) degree? Your area of study (major or program). EXAMPLE: B.A. in Advertising.

- The university (or school) from which you received (or will receive) your degree. EXAMPLE: B.A. in Advertising from Michigan State University

When it comes to *Work Experience*, what we mean is experience based on something you were paid to do. *Additional Experience* falls within the realm of what you have been involved in and/or volunteered for. Remember to include those items that are somehow relevant for or connected to the job you are seeking.

For *Additional Skills*, make sure you read the job ad or announcement carefully. Identify what they are looking for, then add those skills only if you have them. If you don't, and you really want the job, put yourself in a position to start to obtain them (you can always write, *"Currently taking a course to learn xyz ..."*

Too many times people put skills that are good to have, but might not connect to or be needed for the job they are seeking. Skills that are always of interest to most organizations would include language skills. If you speak multiple languages, whether you state that you are bilingual, fluent, advanced, intermediate or beginner level, it is a good idea to let them know. Today, speaking more than one language can open more doors for you professionally than almost anything else on your CV.

When it comes to *Awards & Honors*, not everyone has won something (or won anything that matters or connects to the job they are applying for). For those who have, it is important to share the right kinds of awards or honors; an award for "Selling the most boxes of cookies for class trip in the 9th grade" is not something you need to share on a CV when you are trying to find a job right after graduating from college. It may have helped you land a summer job when you were 15, but now it's time to take it off your CV. However, if you have a relevant award or honor, by all means include it on your CV. It's like having a built-in reference, where you are recognized as being very good at something or you have been recognized for having accomplished something that was above and beyond what others did. Remember, it's not bragging if you can back it up!

Your CV should always end with a line about your *References*. If there is limited space, use the heading "References," then below it write, "References available upon request." Otherwise, if there is space, include the name and contact info for at least 2–3 references right there on your CV. You should leave it up to those who will contact your references to do so on their terms, so make sure you include a complete mailing address, telephone number, and current email address. Most references are contacted on the phone, but it's better to provide complete contact information either way.

What makes someone a good reference?

As we discussed in Chapter 6, *Networking Brand YOU*, you need to find at least 3–5 positive references for yourself, and they need to fulfill the following five requirements for being a good reference or someone who can write a solid letter of recommendation for you:

1. **They know you *professionally*:** They are able to speak of how you worked for them *or* with them, and they can be some type of judge on your ability to deliver results. Remember, a Reference or someone who writes a letter of recommendation does not always have to be someone who is "higher up". It can be someone who has worked with you or even for you.

2. **They know you *personally*:** This means that they know something about your PERSONALity. They must be able to demonstrate that they know you as a person (see next two items to add to this).

3. **They know your STRENGTHS:** A good reference knows some things about you that are positive – otherwise what's the point!? Ideally, they should be prepared to discuss or write about 3–5 words/ short phrases to describe you in a positive light.

4. **They know your WEAKNESSES:** They know some things about you that are *negative*, but you should talk this over with them, as you want them to volunteer the right kinds of weaknesses. These weaknesses should be communicated as things you need to work on improving about yourself; some areas for development. They should NOT focus on things that are wrong with you. Almost all references, if called or contacted, will likely get the question, *"If you know this person as well as you say you do, then you must know some things about them that need improvement?"* And they have to be able to answer this question without messing up the job opportunity for you.

5. **They have *strong communication skills*:** In addition to making sure that a reference has strong verbal communication skills over the phone, many references write a letter of recommendation or "Reference Letter" for you, as this could be required by the potential employer. The writing of a letter of recommendation or a reference letter is in itself an important skill.

Make sure your references are aware of your using their contact information and give them a call or send an email each time you apply for a job or new position and use their name as a reference. Let them know about the type of job you are applying for and what you might want them to highlight or focus on should someone contact them.

As previously stated, a reference letter, often referred to as a letter of recommendation, is one of the most important written documents you will hand over to a potential employer. Make sure you have copies available both as a PDF to email them and as printed-on-paper versions that you can provide at the interview if they ask for one. These types of letters can be well written, but are often hurried, or poorly written. Other times, the person tells you, *"You write the letter, then I will read and sign it."* If they are not willing to take the time to do this on their own, then they are not a good reference for you to use.

Either way, if you want to know what to look for in a letter written about you, or if you ever need to write one someday for someone else, here is a basic outline of how such a letter could be written:

- P1 (Paragraph 1): Who you are writing about and how you know them. When first referring to the person you are writing about, write out the person's full name. Put it in **bold italics**, as this helps the brand name stand out a bit more. Do the same in the final paragraph. Otherwise, refer to them within the letter by their first name, or if a more formal approach is required, as Mr. Smith or Ms. Jones.

- P2: How you know the person you are writing about *professionally*. Here you will discuss in what capacity she/he worked for you (or with you). This could be as general as working together at a specific organization for a specific period of time; or it could be within the context of a particular project or activity/event. The idea behind a short paragraph on how you know this person professionally is to demonstrate that this person was asked to deliver X, and they did indeed deliver X.

- P3: How you feel about this person *personally*. In other words, share a few strengths (adjectives or short phrases) that describe their personality in a positive way. Try and avoid general terms or clichés (she's nice; he's a good guy). Focus on why you liked working with them so much, and how that could mean others would like to work with them as well. Use words that describe the positive sides of her/

his personality. Use their first name when possible in these two middle paragraphs, without overusing it.

- P4: This final paragraph is about thanking the reader and letting them know how they can contact you should they have any more questions about this person (again, in this final paragraph, in your last reference to their name, put first name and last name in ***bold italics***).

It is important to realize that most/many references will be contacted, usually over the phone by the prospective employer, and at times by recruiting firms screening candidates before interview are set up at the actual company or organization. In such a phone call about you, the interviewer will ask the person who is recommending you to go into more detail about their relationship to you and their recommendation of you. So their verbal communication skills over the phone are also very important.

Remember that references can, and often should, at times change, depending on the job opportunity you are seeking. Some references you have on a list of potential references might be better than others for a particular job opportunity. And make sure you keep such a list of potential references up-to-date. Keep in touch with them and alert them anytime you use their name and contact information as a reference for a particular job. They are then alerted to that potential phone call and/or the need to possibly update a letter of recommendation for you. Good, solid references are always willing to do these two things for you. Make sure you are willing to do this for others as well, when you are asked someday to be a reference or write a letter of recommendation for someone else.

Just like your list of references, your CV and your cover letter should also adapt to a specific job opportunity you are seeking. One of the biggest mistakes people make when seeking a job is the *one-size-fits-all* mentality when it comes to these very important documents pertaining to Brand YOU in writing. We repeat this once again, as it is one of the most important things you can do to match your brand, in this case your cover letter and CV, to the demands of the employer, as discussed in Chapter 4.

While you can go online and look for sample layouts for many different types of CVs, it is a good idea to try and find out what a good CV would be for the company/organization, or at least the industry they are in, might look like and/or contain. Remember that CV layouts can vary in terms of what they are called (i.e. CV or resume).

They can also vary depending on national culture, industry or even from organization to organization. Try and do some homework to gauge what type of CV or resume the organization you are interested in working for might want. Otherwise, remember to K.I.S.S. (Keep It Short and Simple), just like your cover letter.

For a sample CV layout that includes these main sections, please see Figure 7.2 on the next page. After the figure there will be a series of practical exercises for you to work on regarding communicating brand you in writing

Same heading as cover letter

CV
John Smith

123 Main Street, 972 55 Luleå • TEL: (321)-123-12345 • E-MAIL: JohnSmith@xyz.com

CAREER OBJECTIVE
Write your career objective here: "To use my education and experience to _____
_____.

EDUCATION
2015 –   Write name of area of study type of degree, frm which schoool
            Then perhaps 1–2 lines with a description (if there is space)

2012–2015 Most people go bakc to high school, as it ledt the reader know
            where you came from or grew up and in some cultures what
            you studied.

WORK EXPERIENCE
2015 –   Job title at which company/organization goes here
            Description (1–3 lines), in italics, describing what you worked with

2012–2015 Job title at which company/organization goes here
            Description (1–3 lines), in italics, describing what you worked with

Make sure you adapt each section and each item specifically to the job you are applying for

ADDITIONAL EXPERIENCE
DATE   Title goes here
            Description (1–3 lines), in italics, goes here

DATE   Title goes here
            Description (1–3 lines), in italics, goes here

ADDITIONAL SKILLS
            Language skills: **Computer skills:**
            • Language 1   • Computer skill 1
            • Language 2   • Computer skill 2

AWARDS & HONORS
DATE   Name of Award and who gave it to you
            Perhaps brief description (1–2 lines) in iltalics here

DATE   Name of Award and who gave it to you
            Perhaps brief description (1–2 lines) in iltalics here

If there is space, include references here

REFERENCES
References available upon request

FIGURE 7.2 Sample layout for a typical CV.

Workbook – Chapter 7

EXERCISE 7 A – Find an actual job: Find a job you are actually interested in right now, then do the following

- Circle the skills and other qualifications they are asking for.

- Now check your cover letter and CV – do you describe how you meet what they are asking for?

- Describe how your CV shows quantifiable results and examples of how you have used these skills in your past.

EXERCISE 7 B – Develop a cover letter

Write a letter that connects to the job opening you found in Exercise 7 a. On your computer, or with pen and paper, outline and begin to write a cover letter using the Four P method.

- PARAGRAPH 1 (P1): Tell the reader what you are writing in reference to. Make a connection to the job being offered and why you are applying for it.

- P2: Tell them why you are right for the job professionally. Here you want to highlight a few items from your CV. Don't go into too much detail, as you can save that for the CV or your interview. Good items to highlight are your **education** and your **experience**, and describe them as they relate to the job being offered. Use power words, or words that the employer uses in the advertisement or description of the job being offered.

- P3: Tell them why you are right for the job personally. Again, lift out and present a few adjectives that others use to describe you (your personality) in a positive way. These are your true **strengths**. Again, connect your strengths to what they are looking for in the job description.

- P4: This is your closing. Use it to thank the reader and push them to your CV. A common way to do this would be to simply write:

"Thank you for your time and consideration with my application for (or interest in) Job X. I look forward to hearing from you should my enclosed (attached; uploaded) CV meet your expectations." A few simple yet powerful sentences that become a call to action to make them at least curious enough to check out your CV.

EXERCISE 7 B – Begin to outline (or update) your CV

Using any number of online outlines for a CV/resume, or in developing your own using the simple outline provided in this chapter, create the following headings and fill in, with most recent dates first, the following:

- Career Objective (To use my education and experience to …)

- Education

- Work Experience (work you were paid to do)

- Additional Experience (anything you volunteered for)

- Additional Skills (language, computer, etc.)

- Awards & Honors (if you have received any)

- References (simply write "References available upon request" below this heading OR choose to list 2–3 complete references (name, organization, mailing address, telephone number, and email) if you have space to use up on the page.

CHAPTER 8

Communicating Brand YOU in Person

"Think twice before you speak, because your words and influence will plant the seed of either success or failure in the mind of another."

NAPOLEON HILL

Developing yourself as a brand is only half of what adds up to your success. Knowing how to communicate that brand is the other half. The last chapter was about communicating Brand YOU in writing, focusing on how to develop an effective cover letter and winning CV in order to get *invited* to a first interview. This chapter focuses on what happens when you get to that interview or, more specifically, how to communicate Brand YOU in person.

In any form of communication, it is important to remember that it never really matters how we *intend* something to be taken, but we must instead focus on how what we are saying (or writing) can be taken by the person receiving the message. That fine line that often exists between confidence and cockiness; that smile that indicates your sincere happiness vs. your overwhelming nervousness; that safe, sure handshake vs. that sweaty, overbearing one – all of this says something about Brand YOU in person.

Some common ways to prepare for an interview revolve around some simple but important questions: What is it that you want to communicate about Brand YOU? How does this match what they are looking for (Chapter 4)? How can what you are communicating leave a positive, lasting impression of you? How can you make people remember you in a positive way once you have left the room? How can you package yourself in a way that supports what you are trying to communicate? This will be the focus of this chapter.

The words that you choose during any personal communication encounter, whether it is face-to-face in the actual interview, or voice-to-voice over the telephone/on Skype, can convey so much beyond how "perfect" you are on your CV. While your cover letter may lead them to your CV, as discussed in the previous chapter, your CV in turn is really just a means to be called in for an interview. You should see your CV as an invitation to the prospective employer. Your aim is that they will RSVP to your invitation by calling or writing and letting you know they would like to interview you or at least meet you in order to see if an interview is warranted.

Being invited to an interview

But what if you don't hear from them? What should you do? While some employers might appreciate being contacted by the applicant, others will not like this at all. So it's hard to say. Some prefer that you have the courage and wherewithal to take the initiative with some form of follow-up after you have sent in your CV. Our advice here is to check with others who have applied to that organization, or make a general call to HR (Human Resources) to see if it would be ok to follow up with a call after you send in your CV. Most organizations will let you know with a phone call, an email or a written letter in the mail within a 4–6 week period, depending on the number of applicants. Others simply expect you to understand, *"If we don't contact you, it means we were not interested."*

Either way, you are advised to be willing to wait patiently to hear from them. You also need to be sensitive to and have the common sense and common courtesy to understand that, at times, there can be dozens or even hundreds of applicants who have sent in their CV for just a single job opening. If a period of 6–8 weeks goes by and you have not heard anything from them, it is likely they were not interested. Either way, it is important that you do not pressure them or give them more to do. Assume that your cover letter and CV arrived safely. Then assume that, if you are of interest to them, they will let you know.

An exception to not calling them once you have submitted your cover letter and CV is to ask a truly relevant question, but this will likely take place before you send in your cover letter and CV. For example, you might have some questions about the job before you use *your* valuable time to apply for it. Another reason to make contact with those offering the job is if you know them. As one hiring manager told us:

"I received a job application from a person I knew who worked within the same organization as me. The point is, I knew him and he knew me. He never mentioned to me that he would apply, nor did he call me to let me know that he was even interested in the position. I even met this person more than once after he had applied, and he never brought it up. To me that is very strange. He might have been the perfect candidate, but the fact that he applied for the position but did not say anything makes me question his judgment."

So it is recommended that if there is a reason to call the organization it is more likely to be BEFORE you send in your application (cover letter + CV) to either check into the organization or the job opening you are interested in, or to show someone you know who works there that you are interested and that you are planning on submitting your application. Remember what was discussed in Chapter 6: It's 20% what you know, 80% who you know. There is nothing wrong with using your network to help promote Brand YOU.

Each of the many applications that come in for a job opening often consists of a cover letter and a CV (let's call these items "interest packets"), and is generally sent in via one of three ways: In the regular mail; attached to an email (we recommend a PDF version of both the letter and the CV); or digitally uploaded to a website via some form of online application process. Always attach or upload in the format they ask for. Otherwise, use PDF, as what you create is what they will see. As we pointed out earlier, it's important to remember that just opening or downloading and organizing all the cover letters with CVs will take up someone's time. Then someone has to begin to read, analyze and sort them. As a general rule of thumb, such interest packets are sorted into one of three piles:

- **Not interested:** Even at a glance, what you wrote or how you presented things showed them you were not of interest for them. Out of 100 applications for a job opening, at least 50 will instantly end up here.

- **Possible candidates:** Out of the remaining 50, maybe 30–40 end up in this pile, with most of them eventually landing in the first pile.

- **Need to interview:** Either right off the bat, or with a few of them coming from the second (Possible Candidates) pile, they may find 10–20 candidates they feel are worth taking the time to interview.

It is becoming more and more common that you first have to do some sort of general skills test and then the actual interview. Sometimes this is done within the same appointment; usually it involves two separate ones. Sometimes these skills tests are done at home and sent in, or online and submitted. If you show that you have these general skills, they can always train you for any others.

Remember that they will first and foremost look at your attitude in the interview. A highly motivated candidate is what they are looking for. People would rather work with colleagues who have a positive attitude but don't really know how to do the job, rather than work with people who are good at what they do but have a negative attitude or who are simply not nice to work with. So make sure you have a track record of being a nice person to work with.

Remember, almost 100% of employers will contact your references and many will Google you, often before that first interview. Then they will nearly always check you out on social media. This will be discussed more in Chapter 9.

Finally, sometimes potential employers will also check, depending on what is legally accessible or available to them, your health records, your police records, your credit history, and other indicators of your overall reputation and standards within society. However, this can depend on which country you are from, as checking many of these things is not permissible in all parts of the world. Just know they want to check on you as much as they are legally allowed to. So make sure you have a clean record within these areas. If you don't, then work to improve them or be ready to at least deal with them and speak positively and explain anything that might come up at an interview.

The first interview is often just the beginning

The first job interview implies you have passed the first main hurdle, implying that they liked enough of your CV and cover letter to at least want to meet you. No one gets hired off the back of their CV (although many HR departments make this mistake). And very few people get hired after only one interview. If you do, it is more likely you have applied to a smaller company or organization. The rule of thumb: The larger the organization, the more interviews you will have to go through to get the job. You get hired because your CV was good enough to warrant a welcome to a first interview. Then this first interview can evolve into a second interview ... and even a third ... or more.

Before you accept or travel to that first interview, do your homework. Find out more about the company so you are familiar with the industry, the organization, and more specifically the job you are being considered for. Doing this pre-interview homework will allow you to become more familiar with how your education, experience and skills match the demands or needs of the employer (go back to Chapter 4 for more on this). Before you go to this first (or any) interview, think about the following questions to ask yourself:

- How can I best contribute my knowledge, experience, skills and/or characteristics to this organization? How can I show them this at the interview?

- What does the actual job entail or include on a daily/weekly basis? Is this really want I want to spend my time doing?

- Would I be happy in this environment? Do I share the same values as the organization or those working at this organization?

Remember that, once you have been contacted to come in for an interview, you can ask the following questions:

- How is the interview structured?

- Who will I meet?

- Should I bring anything that you may want to take a look at?

- Approximately how long will the interview last?

Adhering to the *"Have it and not need it vs. Need it and not have it"* way of thinking is always a good idea. So make sure you ALWAYS bring copies of diplomas, lists of references, grading transcripts, and any portfolio material (e.g. examples or samples of work you have done, if that is important for the job you are interviewing for). Even if they say that you don't need to bring anything, better safe than sorry. It will make a good impression to be ahead of things and offer them up after the interview, as they sometimes remember something they would like a copy or sample of during the interview itself.

Types of interviews

There are many different types of interviews. Sometimes you will only do one type of interview. Other times an organization will have you go through a series of different kinds of interviews or meetings to let them get to know you and see if you really are the person they are looking for. However, there tends to be three main stages to each of these types of interviews:

1. **Pre-interview:** From when you wake up to when you arrive at the address where the interview will take place.

2. **The interview:** From when you enter the place where the interview will take place through the moment you exit that place, be it a building, a part of a building, or a specific office or location within that building.

3. **Post-interview:** Once you have left, this is what happens when you begin to evaluate and think about how the interview went and what the next step will be for that particular job interview.

A normal interview is not always the perfect means for predicting how a person will perform. So more and more organizations are providing exercises, tests, and other challenges for candidates that measure the talents or strengths of the person being interviewed more objectively. And whether it is at the first or the last interview, many organizations require that you somehow mingle with or meet those you will be working with. They then interview those people to see how they think you will contribute, fit in, and could become a strong (or weak) part of their team, or their "family."

There are many types of interviews that can take place for a single job applicant. This goes beyond the first interview vs. second interview, etc.

Interviews can be conducted in person, through information technology (for example Skype), implying there are many ways that an interview can take place either face-to-face or voice-to-voice.

Keep in mind that there are formal interviews, informal interviews, improvised interviews, individual interviews, and group interviews. There are interviews that take place over coffee or lunch, interviews that will take place in an office or conference room, and even those that might have you sitting in a bean bag chair! Because you are not often aware of these types of context (where and how the interview will take place) until you show up, we present some of the more common types of employment interviews when it comes to WHO you might meet below:

- *The interview: One-to-one* – One person interviews you at some stage of the interview process. This is often at the beginning, using someone from HR (Human Resources) or someone from a recruitment firm to screen or weed out applicants. The idea here is to show how you are able to meet or even exceed the demands of the employer/job opening.

- *The interview: Many-to-One* – More than one person from the company in a room at the same time, interviewing you as a group. This often takes place at a second or third interview. Within this group, they might play different roles: The Gatekeeper, who will bring you into the interview and introduce you to everyone; the Influencer, who might be there to provide his or her thoughts on you as a candidate; the Decision Maker, who will ultimately say yes or no to hiring you or passing you along to yet another interview; the Administrator, who is there to take notes and even possibly audio or video record the interview session (more common if you are asked back to a second or third interview). This could also involve you meeting your potential coworkers (or a select group of them). Sometimes employers make their decisions partially on how you come across to those you will end up working with. Do they see you as a worthy teammate?

- *The interview: Many-to-many* – This is often the scenario where you will be working with others who are also interested in the job (fellow applicants) while being observed by others (those doing the hiring). This could involve such tests as solving a case study with a group of applicants; other team exercises or group discussions to see how you interact with others and which role you play in a group (e.g. Are you a leader or a follower? A talker or a listener? Do you focus on the problem or the solution? Are you a time manager or time spender?). This can also be some form of focus group interview, where a moderator and others will sit in, listen to and observe a group of applicants discussing some specific topics that were brought up by the moderator.

- *The interview: One-to-Many* – This is you being asked to give a presentation or see how you might be in a public speaking type of situation. This can often be a late-stage interview, where they want to put you in an actual job scenario and see how you perform. It can also include certain types of role playing, seeing how you react and interact with others in specific situations that are commonly faced by that organization on a day-to-day basis.

The *one-to-one interview* is perhaps the most common and most expected form of interview when trying to get that new job. It is often the first interview that is conducted, either by the organization dong the actual hiring, or by a recruitment firm or employment agency hired by the organization to weed through what can often be interest in a job that has dozens or even several hundreds of CVs and cover letters coming in. This is a time-consuming undertaking for any organization. At times this is done over the phone (voice-to-voice), but it can also evolve from that into a face-to-face meeting.

As we stated earlier, interviews in themselves are not always a perfect predictor of a candidate's true potential. Today, more and more organizations are using various methods to be able to predict more accurately the future performance potential of someone they would like to hire. There are many personality tests that organizations use, as presented in Chapter 3.

While a one-on-one interview is often a first interview, if you pass that one, you might be sent on to a second interview at a later date. Often, this interview is the *one-to-many interview*, which provides a series of new dynamics, where the setting can be varied in many different ways. Many organizations want to see you in a one-on-one setting, but how do you perform in a one-to-many situation? Here there are many ways for you to be tested without really knowing it. Make sure you are P&P (*Polite & Professional*) at all times, to all you who are there.

Being P&P means knowing how to behave in the setting you are in. Being polite means simple manners that, too often, people forget: Showing up on time; not chewing gum; not slurping your water or coffee; not chewing with your mouth open or speaking with food in your mouth (if it is offered or the interview is being done over lunch). It involves many non-verbal cues such as how to sit, stand, and, in general, behave, which will be discussed in more detail later in this chapter under "Non-verbal communication."

Being nice means smiling and staying positive, no matter what they throw at you, figuratively speaking, of course. Some interviews might plant a "good cop vs. bad cop" scenario on you, whereby one person asking you questions will be nice and keep things positive, while the other person, together or in a separate instance, will be rude, combative, and try and push you to become upset or defensive, all while testing to see if you can remain polite and professional, since you might have to deal with customers behaving in a similar fashion. Many times you are being tested, while at other times someone who is interviewing you simply might be rude. But always err on the side of the former – i.e. you are being monitored and tested on how you react to certain situations or types of people.

Being *professional* means showing respect to and making eye contact with *everyone* in the room. Eye contact with someone demonstrates that you are listening and engaged in the conversation. Remember to treat everyone the same, as you never know who is a true influencer as opposed to who is the final decision maker or who is just a casual observer. Common mistakes[1] outlined by many employers include:

---

1 FROM: www.youtube.com/watch?v=R53BYmVDgB8&feature=player_embedded (ACCESSED: August 15, 2016).

- Arriving late
- Misspelling something on your cover letter or CV
- Mispronouncing something during the interview
- Lack of eye contact
- Not being yourself/showing who you really are
- Not answering the question(s) being asked
- Not understanding the role you are applying for or the nature of the organization and the industry within which it exists
- Speaking in vague generalities rather than specifics
- Lack of ability to relate the skill set you say you have with a specific example where you actually used it (and how things resulted by doing so)
- Becoming defensive or acting as a know-it-all type of person
- Talking negatively about others you have worked with or about previous employers (if you have bad feelings, keep them to yourself!)

Always end on a positive note

Almost every interview ends the same way: *"Do you have any questions for us?"* Answering *"No,"* or not being able to come up with at least one relevant, intelligent question could either indicate that you can't think on your feet or that you don't care. And very often, people ask questions that it is actually not a good idea to ask, especially at the first interview: *"How much will I make?* (This can come up at a later interview or after you have been offered the job)? *Do I get an expense account/company car/smart phone/administrative assistant? Can I have Wednesday afternoons off, like medical doctors, to play a round of golf? Am I expected to be here every day, 8–5?"*

Instead, some good questions for you to consider asking, according to Forbes.com[2], could include:

2 FROM: www.forbes.com/sites/nextavenue/2014/06/18/10-job-interview-questions-you-should-ask/ (ACCESSED September 22, 2014).

- What is the single largest problem facing the organization?

- What have you enjoyed the most about working here?

- What constitutes success in this position and at this organization?

- Do you have any hesitations about my qualifications?

- Do you offer continuing education and professional training?

- Can you tell me about the teams I will be working with?

- What can you tell me about your products and plans for growth?

- Who previously held this position?

- What is the next step in the process?

If, in the end, they should decide to go with another candidate, which will eventually happen to all of us in what is a highly competitive job market in most industries within many societies, then accept it and move on. It does not necessarily mean that your interview went badly or that you lacked the skills needed. It just meant that someone else may have had connections within the company, more experience, a larger network or something different or better to offer them than you did.

Always end by shaking hands, smiling, and letting them know that you are still interested in their organization, should there be openings in the future. You want them to remember you as positive even when faced with rejection. Many times, a rejection will come via a phone call or simple email. Other times you could be told face-to-face at the interview, but this is less common. Other times they simply expect you to understand that if you don't hear from them within a specified period of time, it means they went with someone else.

While there is a lot to prepare for before the interview, and there can be many types of interviews to be prepared for, there is one thing that all of the above have in common: Your communication skills. These communication skills can be broken down into two very important areas:

- Your *verbal* communication skills

- Your *non-verbal* communication skills.

However, your ability to communicate in words is only part of what you are communicating to any target audience, be that audience one person, a small group, or a larger audience. Conventional wisdom dictates that up to 60% of what we actually communicate to others is from non-verbal communication, or everything else we convey other than the words we use. One way to look at it comes from an article on the "Four Minutes That Get You Hired"[3]:
The effect or impact our message has comes:

- 7% from the words we use
- 38% from how we say those words
- 55% from our body language and facial expressions

In an online article in Psychology Today, Jeff Thompson actually discusses how this 55/38/7 rule depends on the context, and that a better way to generalize is based on a simpler, 60/40 rule[4]: Up to 60% of a message is conveyed in facial expressions vs. 40% for the vocal components. Either way, non-verbal communication, both facial expressions and also body language, is vital when you are put in the position of meeting someone in a face-to-face context.

For the remainder of this chapter, we will now cover these two vital areas in terms of communicating Brand YOU in person: The words you choose to use and how you share them, as well as the incredible importance of non-verbal communication

Verbal communication: The words you use

Verbal communication is based on the words that come out of your mouth during an interview. However, in the competitive environment of any given job opportunity, your verbal skills might be put to the test in other ways. Your verbal communication skills can be judged within any of the following contexts when you are out trying to get a job:

---

3 Glaser and Smalley (1993). Four Minutes That Get You Hired, *Reader's Digest*. August 1993, pp. 129–132.
4 AVAILABLE: www.psychologytoday.com/blog/beyond-words/201109/is-nonverbal-communication-numbers-game (ACCESSED: October 1, 2015).

Imagine you arrive for a second interview and are called into a room. When you walk into the conference room, three people are sitting on one side of the table. You have not met any of them before. You only know that your cover letter and CV created enough interest for you to get a phone call that took you to that first, often brief, one-on-one interview with a recruiting firm or perhaps someone from human resources within the organization. Now, for the first time, you have been passed along to this second interview, which will often take place with people within the organization who have a higher degree of influence or decision-making power. It is most often these people who are doing the hiring and will really begin to dig a bit deeper to discover the real Brand YOU.

Perfect your "elevator pitch"

The first question at an interview will often be, *"So tell us a little about yourself"*. To prepare for this you should develop what is called the elevator pitch. The elevator pitch is really quite simple, but needs to be thought out and rehearsed in advance of meeting others, especially in interviews (but without sounding rehearsed). The idea is that if you met someone important in an elevator, someone who could help you advance your career, taking around 30–60 seconds to do so (the length of an elevator ride), how would you answer the following question: *"It's nice to meet you, Madeleine, can you tell me a little bit about yourself?"*

Your elevator pitch is a short presentation of Brand YOU. It focuses on allowing you to share your strengths, your current work, your education, a current project, or something else you want to share with someone. It is about simply yet quickly saying something about your achievements, what you are passionate about, and what you want to be doing in the near future. Other than in an interview, an elevator pitch is also an excellent way for you to break the ice and introduce yourself to someone in a professional setting.

Very often, people are not prepared for such an open-ended question as *"Can you tell me a little about yourself?"* and therefore nervously respond, *"Ummmm ... I don't know"*, or, *"What would you like to know?"* Another risky response is to go into too much detail and ramble on a bit too long. These types of response are likely not going to help you very much. See it more as a form of speed dating. You have X number of minutes (or seconds) to convince someone that YOU are an interesting person, or, if asked in a job interview, that you could be the one they are looking for. This elevator pitch is used in order to highlight Brand YOU and establish that all important *positive* first impression.

Other pitfalls in handling a question like this include coming on too strong or becoming the person who tries to sell themselves too aggressively. It's not easy to sound confident without running the risk of sounding like someone who has a bit of an ego problem. Instead, you want to come across as nice, well-mannered and hard working. You want to focus your pitch on PROFESSIONAL You.

So focus your answer primarily on your education, work experience and your skill set, especially as it matches what they are looking for. This is not the art of small talk. It is the ability to win someone over in the first 30 seconds of a conversation. This first 30 seconds sets the tone for the entire interview and often falls prey to what is known as the Halo Effect.

A halo is that ball or circle of light above an angel's head. That being said, what it means is very simple when it comes to how you start any relationship, be it personal or professional: If you start off a relationship negatively, or by coming across in a negative way, even if unintentional, you can do brilliant things later, and you will still be a jerk. But if you start off a relationship positively, you can make mistakes later, and you will be forgiven, as you are considered an angel. It is very important to think about this halo effect in those first 30 seconds when you meet someone for the first time in a professional setting or walk into a room for an interview, where you sit down and often get that most common starting question: *"So, tell us a little bit about yourself"*.

Then use no more than those 30–60 seconds to convey to the listeners just enough about yourself that you seem both intelligent yet personable. Here are some examples of strong elevator pitches:

> **TED:** "I am currently studying for my bachelor's degree in Program X at University Y. I am on schedule to graduate in June 2018. Studying on this program has given me the chance to work with both creativity and problem solving as it relates to developing comprehensive marketing communication campaigns. The connection between the courses and doing work for actual clients within those courses has provided me with additional experience in teamwork, public speaking, and in developing my people and communication skills."

JAN: "I am a graphic designer with experience in printing, web design and application design. My passion is typography and education. I am currently looking for an opportunity in the publishing industry with a focus on developing course literature."

LYNDA: "I have just graduated from Luleå University of Technology with a Master of Science degree in industrial management, with a major in marketing. My thesis work focused on the marketing communication of capital equipment in industrial markets. My passion is to continue to work with marketing communication for a large industrial firm in Sweden or abroad."

Besides starting off with *"Tell us a little about yourself"*, where you can use your elevator pitch, most interviews contain the same types of questions, including the following:

- **What do you know about our company/organization?** It is very important that you are prepared and able to respond intelligently to this question. Keep the answer short and simple, but demonstrate to the person(s) listening that you know something about the company – focus on finding their vision or mission statement. You can learn most about an organization through their website and especially through something like an annual report, if you can get your hands on a copy.

- **Why do you want this job?** With this question the employer wants to know why you want to work with them. They want to see if you are passionate about the job. Prepare by reading carefully about the position and the employer. Articulate specifically why you want the job. But be careful to not connect to what the job will give you, but instead focus on what you will deliver to them (i.e. what they stated they were looking for in the original job ad).

- **Are you applying for other jobs right now?** With this question the employer is trying to gauge just how interested you really are. It is fine if you tell them that you are applying for other jobs. But again, go back and repeat a couple of reasons why you want this job. They are trying to see the risk of you refusing or even leaving their job opening if you are offered something else. Simply put, show that you are genuinely interested in *their* job.

- **What do you think is important to consider in this job?** They want to see how versed you are in the industry and how well-informed you are about the type of work you would be doing at their organization. Don't make things up, which goes back to repeating: Do your homework on this organization and the industry they are in.

- **What can you contribute?** Prepare for this question by thinking about your unique strengths. While your education and experience count for a lot, they can see that on your CV. Focus more on your transferable skills and again connect to some of the criteria for what they are looking for from the job ad. Feel free to volunteer perhaps one or two additional benefits of hiring you, even though they might not be looking for those things – but they could benefit from them.

Using your voice: HOW you say things

Many people tend to go through an odd metamorphosis with their voice when they enter stressful situations. Some things to think about with regards to this include:

- VOLUME: How even can you keep the volume of your voice? Do you become a quiet talker or loud talker when you start speaking in stressful situations? Do you tend to taper off at the end of sentences so it is harder to hear you at certain times?

- PITCH: Some people have high, squeaky voices; others have low, deep voices (and everything in between). Pitch is connected to the type of voice you have right now, and there is not much you can do about that now. But pitch can also be connected to a woman having a little-girl voice or a guy trying to be too macho in how he speaks. Find your best professional voice, which includes keeping how you speak to someone positive, direct, and even.

- TONE: Do you speak up to people, holding them in such high regard that you keep yourself down, "worshiping" them because they are in a more powerful position than you? Or do you speak down to people, become condescending and treat people as if they are dumb and you are smart? Tone in these situations is really about finding a way to talk with people rather than to them.

- SPEED: Do you speed up and talk really fast? Or do you slow down so those you are speaking to can hear every sound that every letter in every word makes? Most people speed up in stressful situations, so make sure with this, as with volume, pitch and tone, that you speak in front of others and get their feedback.

You can't change your voice, of course, but you can work on tweaking it a bit if any of the four items above are an issue for you when you speak, especially in stressful situations. You need to be willing to take feedback from people who know you or have listened to you. What is your voice like? What happens to it when you face something stressful (good stress or bad stress)? If you are a student, feedback from a teacher or fellow students is a great way to obtain objective feedback on your presentation skills and your voice.

However, the words we choose to come out of our mouth, and how we use our voice to deliver them, is only part of communicating Brand YOU in person. An even more important form of communication, often overlooked, often forgotten, is the importance of our facial expressions, body language, wardrobe, and other non-verbal forms of communication.

What you don't say: *The importance of non-verbal communication*

It is a common understanding that up to 80% of what we communicate to others is *non-verbal*.[5] This does not discount the words we use, but it makes how we deliver them, and how we look and behave when doing so, that much more important. While some people are aware of the non-verbal cues they give off, and/or are adept at recognizing the non-verbal cues others are giving them, these days it is becoming more challenging to be good at either of these perspectives. Why? Because the average person in the industrialized world of

---

5 AVAILABLE: www.psychologistworld.com/bodylanguage/ (ACCESSED: August 11, 2016).

the early 21st century often spends more time with their face looking *down* into their smart phone, tablet or computer than they do with their face and eyes upward and outward into the world around them.

People often ask, *"How can I get better at recognizing and understanding other people's non-verbal cues?"* Put another way, how can we all become better poker players? The answer is simple: Face up, eyes open and observe the humanity that is all around you. Take the time when you are traveling to observe others in an airport terminal or at the train station or bus stop. When sitting and having to wait for anything, use it as an excuse to lift your head up from your smart phone and use it instead to look at all the "stories" people can tell you, without you ever meeting them. Observe people as they speak: What are their facial expressions, especially the muscles in and around their mouths and eyes telling you?[6]

What follows is not an exhaustive discussion on the importance of all types of non-verbal communication. Instead, it is more of an invitation for you to think about certain things, then use the Internet, your local or school library, or a book store (online or offline) to find out more. All of these items on the list below are actually communicating something about you. And it all begins before you even come close to opening your mouth to utter the first words that form the answer to their first question. Non-verbal communication, within the context of a job interview, or in fact any social interaction, is made up of a series of cues that we give off via several different situations, as outlined next.

---

6 For more on learning about body language and nonverbal communication, simply Google *"essentials of body language"* or *"nonverbal communication."* You can also do the same on more specific websites such as ted.com or youtube.com.

Bodily Functions

First of all, make sure you give yourself time to "take care of business" and use the restroom or freshen up before you walk into a job interview. Leave yourself at least 30 minutes before the interview to do this. Then consider some of the problems that so many people have when entering stressful situations: Sweaty palms, creeping blush, bad breath, often due to stress, and dry mouth, which also often makes a strange, sticky sound when you are speaking.

All of these represent some common examples of certain biological reactions that we wish we had more control over. While some of you might have problems with issues like sweating, or getting red blotches on your skin (often neck and chest), think about what you wear and remember to breathe in and out. Overall, just do the best you can to deal with or mask these conditions.

Having time to "take care of business" and feel refreshed and ready before your interview is among the most important things you can do to help you communicate confidence once at the interview. Use a stop by a restroom to not only do this, but wash your hands, cool down your face, have a drink of water, and take time to make a "power pose".

What is a power pose? To prepare for such nervous moments as those we face in a job interview, Professor Amy Cuddy from Harvard University conducts research on what she calls the "power pose". According to Dr. Cuddy, before an interview, find a quiet space (e.g. lobby, elevator, restroom); plant your feet widely beneath you; stretch your arms out over your head, making a large V shape (known as the "winner's pose", or "V for Victory!"); hold the pose for 1–2 minutes, as this will actually induce hormonal changes and give you a boost in confidence for your interview.[7] See the woman in Figure 8.1 as an example of a power pose.

7 AVAILABLE: www.inc.com/business-insider/amy-cuddy-the-poses-that-will-boost-your-confidence.html (ACCESSED June 15, 2016); or just go to ted.com or youtube.com and put in "Amy Cuddy" for some excellent tips on non-verbal communication.

FIGURE 8.1 The Power Pose. PHOTO BY: Melina Granberg.

One of the worst things you can do in an interview is end up running late, get to your destination out of breath, not have time to take care of business and walk in sweaty, stressed, and sloppy. Better to be "cool, calm and collected" than "sweaty, stressed and sloppy" any day of the week.

Once you are ready, then be at the office or the place you need to be at least 15–20 minutes early and fix your schedule for things to run late. Remember, you are adapting to their schedule, not the other way around. Better to be 30 minutes early for an interview than 3 minutes late.

Waiting to be called in for the interview

So you have "taken care of business" and refreshed yourself a little. Now it's time to get to the exact location of the interview and wait. Let's say you are waiting in the lobby, or perhaps an outer office, waiting to be called into a conference room or into someone else's office. How you sit, stand, interact with others while waiting, or even just how you sit and behave by yourself can have two implications. First, think that this is actually being observed by someone. Approach this by acting as though you are "ON" the minute you walk into the physical location (building or room) where you will be waiting for the interview to take place. Second, while this might seem like a minor detail to some, and it is not likely that many organizations have the time or resources to observe you in such situations as when you are waiting to come in for the interview, how you wait to be called in to another room also affects your own behavior and ultimately your confidence and performance in that interview.

Such tense moments as waiting to be called in can lead to either making you more nervous or less nervous, depending on your approach. Remember to sit up straight, breathe in and out, and keep your mind occupied by reading something or checking emails on your smart phone. If there are others there waiting (for an interview or for something else), make eye contact, smile and perhaps engage in some small talk should the opportunity present itself and seem appropriate. If there is any type of gatekeeper (secretary or administrative assistant), make sure you are extra-friendly and professional with them. Yes, gatekeepers will observe you and quite possibly be asked about whether they think you should join their team or not. Never, ever treat anyone as though they are "below" you, regardless of your education, experience, or how impressive your credentials are.

Entrance/Exit

Now your name gets called. Or someone enters that room and comes up to you to see if you are "Jane Doe." How you stand up and greet this person is very important. Then how you enter a room to greet the person or people who are about to interview you is an important non-verbal cue which is vital in terms of forming first impressions, which lean one of two ways: It either leans towards positive or leans towards negative, right out of the gate.

How do you walk in? How is your eye contact? Think about your handshake (e.g. too hard or too soft). Wait for them to invite you to sit down. You are being judged from the second you walk into a situation where other people begin to observe and interact with you. Use the chance to observe them as well, as their body language and facial expressions will tell you what they are thinking. Simply put, your interview begins before anyone ever really begins to speak. Here are a few tips for your entrance into a room:

- Walk in head up, shoulders straight, but not too stiff. Remember to breathe in and out.

- Remember to smile – act like you are happy and comfortable being there.

- Scan the room and make eye contact with everyone there.

- Shake hands/introduce yourself to everyone in the room.

- Unless it is obvious, wait to be told where and when to sit.

- As you sit, take a deep breath and relax. It's a job interview – you are not on trial.

Facial Expressions

Now the interview has begun. Facial expressions have the most direct impact as a non-verbal cue on other people. Why? Because you are often maintaining eye contact with others during a job interview, maintaining a focus on one another's facial cues as a means for truly understanding what the other person is actually communicating. Most of the time this is on a subconscious level, but we all pick up on other people's non-verbal cues, especially when looking at them during a conversation. Muscle movement in your face, especially around the eyes/eyebrows and mouth areas, say so much about you without you having to use words.

How you use the muscles in your face will dictate everything from your mouth (smile or frown) to your eyes (are you trying to recall something or are you making something up?). Do you clench your jaws when nervous? Do your eyes look up or down, left or right when you answer a question or simply think about what was just asked of you?

Very often, we do not realize what we give away in tense, pressure-packed moments (like job interviews or, for that matter, poker games). But if up to 80% of all communication between two people who are facing each other is NON-verbal, then most of that non-verbal communication likely comes from your facial expressions, and from that, the most telling of all facial expressions comes from the use of muscles in and around your eyes.

The old saying *"The eyes are the window to the soul"* actually provides a good example here. In a job interview, it means *"The eyes are the window to the true you."* Your eyes and how you use them speak volumes about you and your personality.

Even if they do not catch every little glitch or tweak, you will still leave them with an impression that can either lean towards a positive feeling about you, or a negative one.

Here are some tips regarding facial expressions and your eyes:[8]

- If you want to show someone you are interested in what they are saying, make eye contact.

- Make sure you make eye contact with everyone in the room or at the table, not just with the person asking the question and/or the person in the room you think has the most power.

- Too much eye contact can be perceived as a threat or make someone feel uncomfortable.

- Lack of eye contact can imply shame or deception. However, looking away to ponder a question and come up with the right answer is normal.

- Eyes that look to the left often indicate that the person is reminiscing or trying to remember something; looking to the right indicates more creative thoughts and might indicate someone trying to make something up (be deceitful or lie). This can be the opposite for left-handed people.

- The pupils of the eye react (shrink and grow) due to a number of factors outside our control, for example the amount of light in the room. However, the less interested someone is, the more their pupils will contract; the more interested, the more the pupils tend to dilate.

It is not just the eyes that can give away what you are thinking or really mean, but the muscles around your mouth can also tell people a lot about what you are thinking or feeling. Mouth movements such as pursing your lips or twisting them to one side can indicate that you are thinking about what you

---

8 AVAILABLE: www.psychologistworld.com/bodylanguage/eyes.php (ACCESSED August 25, 2016).

are listening to or that you are holding something back.[9] Clenching your jaw muscles can indicate stress or the idea that you don't like what you are hearing or have something to hide.

According to bodylanguageproject.com, a common set of non-verbal cues comes from hand-to-mouth gestures. According to this source, hands that come up to cover a mouth or play with one's lips can indicate a lack of confidence and overall insecurity in the person doing it.

Body Language

There are many books and videos on body language and what it means as a form of non-verbal communication. How you sit and wait for someone to call your name to go into a room for an interview; how you walk into that room for the first time; how you approach the person (or people) in that room, arm stretched to shake their hand(s); what your body language and facial expressions communicate during the actual interview.

Here are some things to think about when it comes to body language other than facial expressions:

SITTING: How you sit when being asked to go ahead and sit down has a lot to do with the layout and furniture in the room where the interview will take place, just as the sitting position you take depends on whether you are sitting across the desk from someone; sitting around a table with others; sitting in a chair where no table or desk exists; sitting on a chair, a sofa or a bench. All of this is important to consider. According to businessknowhow. com, simple things like the angle of your body can show more than you think regarding what's going on in your head: Leaning in says "tell me more," while leaning away says "not that interested". Sitting (or standing) erect shows that you are alert and enthusiastic, while slouching or slumping implies lack of energy or lack of interest.[10]

9 AVAILABLE: www.businessknowhow.com/growth/body-language.htm (ACCESSED August 22, 2016).
10 AVAILABLE: www.businessknowhow.com/growth/body-language.htm (ACCESSED: August 26, 2016).

ARMS & LEGS, FINGERS & FEET: Whether you are sitting or standing, how are you using your arms? Are they folded, making you seem defensive by looking bigger than others, which is often a sign of insecurity? Avoid playing with a pen or drumming your fingers on the table or tapping your feet on the floor. Don't sit on your hands or fold your arms. Instead, bring your hands up, clasp them gently and lean in to the table slightly. Let the interviewer know that you are comfortable being there and are tuned in and fully engaged. Leaning away implies disinterest or a wish to escape.

Another sign of not wanting to be there is feet that are pointed somewhere other than at the person interviewing you. Depending on the furniture in the room and where you are asked to sit during an interview, think of this simple idea when sitting (or standing) and talking to someone: *"Flat feet, flat hands!"*

Without coming across as a sort of stiff robot, keeping your feet flat on the floor, firmly planted, gives you a foundation that supports you – both literally and figuratively. This aids in the flow of blood and makes breathing easier. If sitting at a table, then have your hands up on the table, one over the other, or gently clasped. Hands below the table, in your pockets, or behind your back imply you have something to hide or are extremely uncomfortable. Showing that you want to be there comes from making sure you show this with your body language.

The key with arms and hands, legs and feet, is that these appendages often begin to fidget (move around) due to nervousness. If you have a tendency to tap your feet, move your leg, or fiddle with your fingers, then you need to practice not doing these things in stressful situations. Ask a friend or family member to give you a mock interview by going online and Googling or using a social media like Pinterest to find "The 10 Most Common Interview Questions" and let them ask you these questions.

Wardrobe

You are what you wear! Your appearance when it comes to what you wear and how you wear it matters more than most people realize. Wardrobe choices often equate to first impressions, and first impressions are always one of two things: Positive or negative.

Have you done your homework so you know how to dress for the interview (formal or informal)? Do the clothes you wear fit you properly (style; color; fit)? What accessories will you use (jewelry, watch, brief case)? The main advice here is to not overdo it with any of these, but find a way to fit in and make a positive impression with your overall look that connects or relates to the values and way that people at that organization dress.

Think about the following when it comes to your wardrobe decisions:

- What do you want to communicate with your overall appearance? Think about what you need to wear for each type of interview you attend.

- See the clothing you would wear to a job interview or another important function as an investment, not a cost. Save up and spend a bit more on quality items rather than trying to save money and have items of clothing that don't fit properly or look good on you.

- Ask yourself what you need to improve about your look when it comes to style, color, and fashion trends. You need to do your homework here. A great investment is having a professional wardrobe consultation or using a professional shopper in terms of gaining professional, objective advice on the sizes, styles and colors that work best on you. This is as important for men as it is for women. And it should be done at least every few years, if not every year, as your body and looks (fashion trends) change over time.

- Make sure you are not overdressed or underdressed for a specific job interview. There are organizational cultures, or corporate cultures or corporate values that often dictate how people may dress within an organization or entire industry.

- Let common sense guide you: Of course you should never wear dirty jeans, a ratty t-shirt, and a baseball cap worn backwards to an interview. If unsure, dress business casual, with a more conservative look. Conservative is always safer than unconventional or flashy.

- Yes, accessories (jewelry, watches, etc.) count as wardrobe. However, they will now be dealt with in a separate section.

Accessorizing

Your jewelry, including watches, piercings, scarves, and anything else that is not a "pant-shirt-shoe" part of you, is considered an accessory. How can you use such accessories to make your brand appear more professional? Or how can accessories become too much of a distraction or take away from your professional image? You want to be memorable for the right reasons, not the wrong ones, and visual cues such as wardrobe and accessories can be very memorable.

Here are some things to think about when accessorizing:

- **Jewelry**: There is nothing wrong with a necklace, bracelet or simple, pierced ears. But too much of anything, be it based on color, size or amount, can simply become too much of a distraction. It's often about blending in rather than standing out too much when it comes to jewelry, or any accessories discussed here. Better to err on the side of caution than on the side of distraction!

- **Multiple piercings & tattoos:** Think of it this way: That pierced tongue, those multiple piercings up and around your left ear, or those tattoos that cover your upper neck or reach out onto the top of your hands might be you simply wanting to demonstrate your individualism and creativity. They might even have some personal or emotional meaning for you. However, in communication terms, they are considered "noise". Noise is something that gets in the way of the message being delivered. We are not saying you should not be yourself, nor are we saying you should remove or hide things. But you want them to remember you for the right reasons, not the wrong ones. Anything that becomes a distraction *or* that can make people stereotype you based on the way you dress or how you accessorize can get in the way of your getting the job. So the advice here is to do your homework and dress and accessorize in a manner that connects to the values of the organization hiring you – it won't work if you expect them to either take the time to understand or adhere to your values. Remember, you want something from them more than they want something from you.

- **Hair accessories:** Many people, especially those with longer hair, use ribbons, clips and other accessories in their hair to obtain a certain style or to provide a simple function, like keeping their hair out of their eyes or face. Here you need to think about such hair accessories blending in and not dominating your hair. Too big or too bold/bright can be a distraction. You dye your hair purple on Friday to attend a special party for a friend, but have a job interview on Monday morning – you need to decide which is more important. For your friend's party, buy a colored wig instead.

Grooming

Is your hair looking good or did you just get out of bed, not make it into the shower, and have "bed head" (i.e. a section of your hair sticking out or up)? Have you clipped your fingernails properly? Is your make-up just the right amount? Have you avoided using aftershave/cologne or perfume? Did you brush and floss and use a mouthwash?

While the questions above may sound either like common sense or a bit too picky, they should make you pause to consider all the things that can be noticed, and therefore judged, by others when they look at you (as opposed to what you might see when you look at yourself in the mirror). Since your wardrobe will cover up most of you, let's focus on those two parts of your body where grooming is vital in interview situations: Your head/face and your hands (and yes, even how you smell).

Let's illustrate this with the following example from a former police chief, let's call him **Bob**, who came from the Midwestern United States:

> "As police chief, I was usually the final interview. The candidate had obtained the proper education and gone to the police academy. They had passed certain physical, mental and emotional tests. They had gone through some early interviews. If they came to me, it meant they had done well up until that point. I had a standard set of questions to ask each of them, as even when they got to me, there were always more candidates than there were openings for new police officers.
>
> I always had them sit across from me, on the other side of my "Big Chief's Desk," and often a bit lower than where I sat. From this vantage point, I still usually only saw them from the chest up. This meant that their hands were

often down on their lap, as it was not easy to put them up on my desk. So my final question almost always involved putting a pen and paper out in front of them on the desk and asking, "Write down three reasons YOU think I should hire you? You have 60 seconds ...

Well, their hands came up and they started to write. I might look at the answers, but really did not care all that much. What I really wanted to look at (and judge) was their fingernails.

Were they bitten and chewed? That implied a nervous habit. Were they uncut and/or grimy and dirty under the nails? That implied that appearance did not matter – and appearance for a police officer always mattered. Or perhaps they had long extensions, making the nails sharp and dangerous. This meant a lack of attention to detail. Did they not think that, should I hire them and they had to take down a criminal and their nails scraped that criminal's face, my department would be sued? And isn't attention to detail always important for a police officer?

What I learned from a person's hands, and especially his or her finger-nails, did not always mean I would not hire them. But within the context of the interview, it often provided me with the opportunity to dig a little deeper and ask questions based on what I saw. It's one of many things I looked at or observed on the individual."

Here are some simple tips that might seem like common sense, but we share them here nonetheless:

- **Hair**: Think about not having "bed head" (hair sticking up improperly due to not showering or lying down before you arrive for the interview). Be careful not to be too bold or stick out too much with hair coloring or highlights – too bold colors or highlights might not fit in with their corporate look or how they want you to come across to customers, etc. Finally, something as simple as a haircut about a week before is a good way to have things looking trimmed and smart.

- **Face**: Make-up should be neutral and not too heavy. Simple advice here is to blend in rather than stick out. If you tend to blush or become "splotchy", a form of rash that quite suddenly covers parts of your body, especially your chest, neck and arms and is usually triggered by anxiety and stressful situations[11] there are medical and wardrobe tips for how to overcome this problem that many people face.

- **Hands**: First and foremost, take a look at your fingernails! Are they clipped and trimmed properly? Do you tend to chew your nails down to the quick (nervous habit)? Is there grease or grime under them (lack of attention to detail)? It does not matter if your hobby is working on restoring old cars – unless you are interviewing for a job as a mechanic, makes sure your nails are cleaned and trimmed properly. What about nail polish or super-long extensions? Bright, flashy colors should give way to more neutral, business-friendly colors.

- **Smell**: While your clothes should be fresh and you should, of course, shower the morning of your interview, be sure not to overwhelm anyone with too much perfume or cologne/aftershave. In fact, skip wearing any fragrances at all, as if they are "good" they can be a distraction, but very often they are considered a bad thing as people wear too much or are not sensitive to the fact that others might have allergies or there might be policies in place that dissuade or forbid the use of such fragrances. Simple rule: Smell neutral. Another common smell issue is bad breath. Eating that meal last night that contained extra onions and extra garlic will likely not help your chances at an interview the next morning. Think about what you eat the day before, and as stated earlier, floss your teeth, brush your teeth, and gargle with a mouth wash before you go to the interview. If you sit across from someone in an interview with bad breath, it's almost a guarantee the only thing they will remember about you is your (bad) breath!

The discussion above on all these things to think about regarding your non-verbal communication conveys those parts of us that communicate, often very powerfully if not subtly, something about us, without ever using

---

11 AVAILABLE: www.thedoctorstv.com/articles/2848-embarrassing-flushing-triggered-by-anxiety (ACCESSED June 15, 2016).

any words. These non-verbal cues leave a lasting impression on anyone in the room. The people receiving or observing are probably not measuring or paying direct attention to these cues, but all of them seep into the interviewer's subconscious mind and leave a very strong impression, again, either positive or negative, about YOU as a brand.

Use the exercises for Chapter 8 to think about how this applies to you.

Workbook – Chapter 8

This chapter has focused on communicating Brand YOU in person. The focus has been on the types of interview, what to expect at these interviews, and the verbal and non-verbal communication skills needed to succeed in these interviews. Below you will find a series of exercises that can be considered a kind of audit of what communication skills you think you have and those you think you need to work on.

EXERCISE 8 A – Audit the words you use

Develop on paper then practice your elevator pitch.

If someone asked you, *"Tell me a little bit about yourself"*, how would you answer in a way that lasts around 30 seconds (a common length of time it takes to ride an elevator) and makes them interested in you?

Template for preparing your elevator pitch:

Your education: _____

Your current job/title: _____

Your current focus/passion: _____

_____

_____

What you are looking for right now: _____

_____

Now use this to formulate your elevator pitch:

_____

_____

_____

_____

EXERCISE 8 B – Audit your voice (how you say things)

- **Volume**: Do you get quieter or louder when stressed?
- **Speed**: Do you speed up or slow down when stressed?
- **Tone**: Do you talk up or down to people in certain situations? Do you get overly happy or serious when speaking in stressful situations?
- **Pitch**: Does your voice get squeaky or mousy? Do you tend to taper up your speech at the end of a sentence in order to sound more happy or positive? Or does your voice taper up at the end of a sentence or statement to sound more serious?

EXERCISE 8 C – Audit your non-verbal cues

- What do you want to communicate with your overall appearance (e.g. competent, professional, confident, responsible, orderly, creative)?
- To whom are you trying to communicate this (e.g. write down an answer to this for a job you currently have; a job you are interested in or are applying for now; or one that you could be in the near future)?
- What is the context within which you are sharing your "look" with others? For example in a job interview? At a meeting (formal or informal)? Over coffee or lunch (dress code of restaurant)?
- What photos have you posted on social media that you are a part of? What photos have others posted of you? (More of this in Chapter 9).
- What do you know about the organizational culture of the place you are trying to get hired at? Do they have a dress code? In the office vs. meeting with clients?

- On a 5-point Likert Scale, how would you rate the following: (SCALE: 1 = poor; 2 = fair; 3 = good (average); 4 = very good; 5 = excellent)
  - Your handshake
  - Your eye contact
  - Your ability to sit and wait
  - Your ability to sit and have a conversation
  - Your ability to stand and wait
  - Your ability to stand and have a conversation
  - Your table manners (at a restaurant; over coffee or a meal)
  - Your facial expressions (especially muscles around your eyes/ eyebrows and your mouth)
  - Any problems with "splotching" (the rash that often comes in patches on your neck, chest and arms)?

EXERCISE 8 D – Conduct a Practice interview

- Find someone to sit down and ask you some questions that would commonly come up in an interview. We provide a few questions below.

- Record yourself, preferably on video, but at least your voice, answering questions (see sample questions below).

- Evaluate your pitch, volume, tone and speed, as well as the answers you are providing.

EXERCISE 8 E – Practice your answers

While you can Google to find common interview questions, or visit places like Pinterest.com and search for the same, some of the more common interview questions might include but not be limited to:

- Tell us a little about yourself. (NOTE: Remember your elevator pitch)
- What skills do you have to make you a good candidate for this job?
- Are there any skills you feel you lack?
- What is your experience of public speaking?
- How do you tend to go about planning and organizing your work?
- Do you prefer to work alone or in a team?
- What role do you take in a team?
- What makes a team player a team player?
- Tell us about a situation where you had a hard time cooperating with someone and what you did to resolve it.
- Tell us about a conflict you have been part of and what you did to resolve it.
- Tell us how you keep and grow your network.
- What do you do (what habits do you have) that creates strong, professional relationships?
- Would you rather work with deadlines or at your own pace?
- How do you manage stress?
- What stresses you other than deadlines/lack of time?
- How do you plan and prioritize?
- What makes you happy and motivated on the job?
- What do you need in your work environment to keep you motivated?
- What can make you lose your motivation?
- What kind of manager do you need to reach your full potential?

- Tell us about your life outside the office.

- Why should we hire you?

- Why shouldn't we hire you? Name at least one weakness you have. What are some of your weaknesses?

Ask yourself: What do I need to improve on when it comes to any of the items above?

Ask others: Talk to others who are around you a lot and know you well. Perhaps they have seen you in a public speaking or similar situation. Ask them to evaluate how you speak and your non-verbal cues. From their perspective, what could you improve on?

CHAPTER 9

Managing Digital Brand YOU

"Social media is not just an activity; it is an investment of valuable time
and resources. Surround yourself with people who not just support you
and stay with you, but inform your thinking about ways to WOW your
online presence."

SEAN GARDNER[1]

Getting hired in the digital age provides both opportunity and risk. There
is the version of Brand YOU that lives in the bricks and mortar of the real
world. This is the version of Brand YOU that writes cover letters, develops
CVs, and attends interviews. However, there is another version of your
personal brand: The digital version of Brand YOU, the one who resides in the
realms of that online world known as cyberspace. Information technology
and the ever-growing potential of the Internet, which today includes endless
websites, apps and multiple social media options, not only makes everyone
more visible, but everyone becomes a recorder of the people and events
around them as well.

The ways in which you can "show" digital Brand YOU are many and
varied and limited only by the speed of progress within information
technology. Only 20 years ago, we were barely using email. Before that, we
were running to a printing store to make paper copies of our cover letter and
CV to put in an envelope, stamp and seal, and mail off to the organization
we were interested in working for. Your use of information technology in
general, and social media in particular, leaves an impression of Brand YOU

---

1 AVAILABLE: blog.kissmetrics.com/50-social-media-influencers/ (ACCESSED: September
25, 2015)

on multiple levels, with multiple audiences, both personal and professional. This chapter will focus on providing some simple but important tips on how to manage digital Brand YOU on both of these levels.

These digital versions of Brand YOU can come via any or all of the following social media, depending on which ones you use, or which ones others might use or post your name in. Like any website, all social media are today presented and used through websites and/or apps on our smart phones and tablets. Please note that while the following list is not exhaustive, it represents what can be considered the Top 10 social media used today[2]: Facebook, Twitter, Google+, LinkedIn, YouTube, Instagram, Pinterest, tumblr (blogging), Flickr, Skype, Wikipedia – and the list goes on, as new social media pop up regularly and existing social media find ways to constantly update and improve. This list can of course vary depending on which part of the world you live and work in.

For our purposes, the idea is not to cover all of these social media, but select a few examples (types) of these social media and provide some tips on what to think about as you build this cyber version of yourself, or what we refer to as Digital Brand YOU. What we discuss for one social media can likely be considered for any of the websites and social media that you use today.

Keep in mind that when it comes to social media, the three levels of Brand YOU apply: Private You, Personal You, and Professional You (see Chapter 3). The advice here is to really take a look at what you are leaving out there, or what others are saying about you, on all social media. Regarding Private You, that should be left where it belongs – in private! Once you put something (or someone else puts something) about you out there in cyberspace, it is no longer private. Personal You can certainly be a part of social media, so long as it reflects positively on Brand YOU.

---

2 AVAILABLE: www.pewresearch.org/data-trend/media-and-technology/social-networking-use/ (ACCESSED: December 30, 2013).

Start by Googling yourself

Your journey into cyberspace, to really understand Digital Brand You, begins with Google. Or to put it another way, you need to Google yourself. When you do this, consider that you might have a more common first and/or last name, so it sometimes helps to Google yourself using an additional descriptor to your name. For example, instead of just Googling, "Sue Smith" (fictional name for demonstration purposes only), try Googling "Sue Smith, Name of City"; or "Sue Smith, Company or School name." This will help Google narrow its hits to a more specific focus on you. This should also include online names you might use, for example, google your Twitter handle (e.g. @timfos or @mia_oldenburg).

You will be amazed at what you find. Has someone mentioned you in one of their blogs? Has your name appeared in a newspaper or magazine article? Has someone posted a picture or comment about you on Facebook or Twitter? Has a video been shot and uploaded to YouTube, with your name mentioned? What public and private information is out there with Brand YOU a part of it or at least being mentioned? For that matter, what professional information is out there about you? Is it accurate? This should include another social media, *Wikipedia.com*, where you can not only be written about, but you can add content to postings as well.

Even if the actual website or social media where you were mentioned or to which you were somehow connected no longer exists, it can still be found within Internet archives such as https://archive.org. A good rule of thumb to not only guide your future actions, but look over any past actions on the Internet: *"Once in cyberspace, always in cyberspace."*

And while you don't always have control over what others post about you, you can maintain a degree of control by keeping up with your settings on various social media. Do you have to "o.k." a photo or comment using your name? If you find something that you are mentioned or tagged in, can you "un-tag" yourself, or ask someone to do the same? The very essence of any and all social media is that they are in fact designed for people to connect to, mention, and interact with other people. But everything that uses your name or image out there in cyberspace can be discovered by others, and you can bet employers are investigating "digital Brand YOU" before they hire you. In fact, they are likely doing it before they bother to even bring you in for the first job interview. If these organizations don't investigate your digital fingerprint themselves, there are companies today that specialize in investigating you this way on behalf of these employers. While we will not mention or endorse any such companies here, simply Google or use another search engine and ask the question: *"Are there companies that investigate your social media?"*

Employers today are doing this for many reasons. They want to see if you are a likeable person. They want to see if what your CV says matches who you really are. They want to see if there are any risks or downsides to potentially hiring you. Will your personal brand hurt their brand as an employer? Do you share the same values that they do as an organization? Some companies even use this information to come up with more specific questions for you at the job interview.

What if you discover something negative about yourself out there in cyberspace? What if you find an unflattering or untrue comment? What if there is a photo or video with you in it that might hurt your reputation or how someone else might perceive you? Remember, it does not matter how something is intended, what matters is how someone else takes what they are reading or seeing. For example, your friend at that party last month meant it only as good fun when they posted a picture of you with a lampshade on your head, party streamer in your mouth, and bottle of beer in your hand as they wrote about you on their blog, on their Facebook page, via Twitter, or any other social media. In fact, you were not only sober, you were just playing along to give them a good pic. But that employer who discovers this photo of you can only see it as a potential problem. Are you a party-lover who often gets drunk? Do you have a drinking problem? Are you unreliable, unprofessional and unpredictable?

And the further your career advances, the more important this becomes. We have all seen politicians running for office, only to be "called out" or "discovered" doing something or saying something that is either a mistake on their part or is simply misinterpreted or misrepresented. When it comes to the old adage *"There is no such thing as bad publicity,"* forget about it. There absolutely *is* such a thing as bad publicity, or bad information.

When it comes to Brand YOU, digital or in the real world, you want to be perceived as a worthy candidate. You want to be perceived as someone who will not only exceed expectations, but never become a risk for the organization hiring you. And a risk is now anything you have done in your past that can be shared on any number of social media. Whether it's a company interested in hiring you or the mass media (a journalist) checking on something involving you, among the first things they will do is check your social media profiles and Google you for anything that might provide additional information or perspectives on what they are trying to find out.

As the manager of a small business told us:

> "In my hometown we all remember a once successful businessman who actually lost his job due to what he posted on Facebook. This included photos he had posted and groups he had joined or pages he had 'Liked.' The owners of the company thought this was hurting their brand and it ended up receiving a lot of negative media coverage as well. In this town, at least, his career is over. He can't get hired."

Let's say you are none of these – i.e. it does not matter because you only post things on those social media you use that are positive in nature. But what are others posting about you? You need to learn to consider the idea that everyone out there, while probably not out to get you or hurt your reputation, is like some kind of pseudo-journalist. Most people are not only walking around with cell phones (smart phones) that contain digital cameras, video cameras and a built-in keyboard, but they can take that picture, record that video, write about it and POST it in an almost instantaneous fashion to any number of social media. Without scaring anyone off from using this wide array of amazing social media that is available today (and new ones certainly arriving in the future), it is important to note that, while they provide countless benefits, they do have some potential drawbacks. To address this, what follows are a few tips for the main social media available today, starting with the social media that really counts for professional Brand YOU: LinkedIn.

LinkedIn: *How to really communicate Brand YOU*

If you are reading this and currently do not have a LinkedIn account, STOP reading and go create one (www.linkedin.com). Come back here only after you have at least opened up a LinkedIn page about yourself. LinkedIn is the online version of a more dynamic, interactive CV for Brand YOU. It is perhaps one of the most important developments in early 21st-century social media, especially as it applies to professional Brand YOU.

While most CVs today are sent in as a PDF, attached to an email or uploaded on a website, there are still many advantages to developing a solid LinkedIn page. It is important to understand that this digitalization of our CV will likely become, or already is, the future of developing and sharing our CV within many organizations. Corporate and organizational sustainability efforts are pushing for more eco-friendly, green initiatives, including leaving less of a carbon footprint. Think of the number of trees it takes to develop the millions of paper-based CVs produced around the world each year, which also require the envelopes to mail them in, not to mention the Co^2 emissions being used to deliver them by air, land and sea. Simply put, stop what you are doing right now and go to Linkedin.com to start your online CV right now. Here are a few suggestions and tips for you to consider as you do:

- For your career, LinkedIn is more important than all of the other social media combined. Start your page TODAY; update it often; manage it carefully.

- It is a dynamic, interactive online CV that allows you to post and keep things updated in a much simpler way than dealing with the paper-based CVs that are becoming outdated but not unheard of.

- It allows you to be recommended for certain skills, with any number of individuals either nominating you for a particular skill or endorsing you for having that skill.

- It allows for recommendation letters (or statements) to be posted by specific people. You can proactively ask others to do this for you or reactively approve a recommendation someone has written for you.

- LinkedIn also enables you to have others find you and offer you a job. You can search for job opportunities geographically, by industry, or even with specific organizations. With LinkedIn, it is not just one (you) to many (the organizations), but now organizations are using it to find you as well.

- For those of you who have graduated from college, pages such as LinkedIn's alumni search is a very useful tool, as you can see where other graduates are located, which companies they are working for, their current and past job titles and so on. It's also a great way to network with people from your alma mater and or connect to people in industries or companies/organizations that you might like to work for some day.

- You can use LinkedIn to investigate others and what they have done to reach a position similar to the one you are seeking. What did it take for them to get there in terms of their listed education and experience?

- You could take this one step further and send them a private message via LinkedIn. You would be surprised how many people will take a few minutes to help a stranger reach their career objective(s).

- Remember that LinkedIn is also used as a global head-hunting tool for recruitment by companies for their job openings. If you are not there, how can they find you?

- Once you join, choose to belong to (or follow) certain groups or individuals who post information or articles on LinkedIn. This will help expand both your network and your knowledge.

- Use LinkedIn to investigate organizations you might consider working for. This is especially important, as not only can they use LinkedIn to check up on you, you can use it to check up on them. This makes you even more prepared for any potential interview.

While LinkedIn is the social media for *Professional* Brand YOU, most of the other social media are connected to *Personal* Brand YOU. We discuss those next.

How other social media can help or hurt you

Other than LinkedIn, there are of course many other social media that are used by individuals for both personal and professional reasons. Today, people, companies, organizations, brands – so many have a Facebook page, a Twitter account, a blog to read. Our focus here will be on *your* use of some of the more popular social media that exist today, starting with what is probably the most famous and most used of all social media, Facebook.

Facebook

So many people use a Facebook page (Facebook.com) to connect and interact with primarily friends and family. That is what it was originally intended for. We often now include people from work, people we meet within our work, as well as casual acquaintances (people we have met but might not consider a true friend).

Other than LinkedIn, Facebook is the ultimate networking social media. However, unless you "block" someone, anyone can visit the start page (public version) of your Facebook page. This implies you should check your privacy and security settings on your Facebook page and click on the option "This is what others see" when they click on your Facebook profile. Either way, it's important to know that social media such as Facebook can help and/or hurt Brand YOU. Here are some more specific tips and things to think about when it comes to Facebook and Brand YOU:

- **To Like or not to Like:** These days, companies, organizations, political parties, religious institutions and the majority of major corporate, product and service brands use Facebook. You can "Like" or "Join" an infinite number of Facebook pages or groups, respectively. Each one of these Like or Join buttons that you click on communicates something about you. So it's really not just about your Facebook page, but the pages you Like and Join as well. People have actually been fired for their Likes on Facebook, the groups they belong to, as well as what they post themselves (comments or photos).

- **It's social:** Remember that the key word in social media is SOCIAL, which means people can not only be exposed to it, but they can "Share" it as well. Add to this the idea of listing your favorite movies; your favorite books; where you have traveled. The list of things you can share with the rest of the world on Facebook seems never-ending.

- **How can Facebook help you?** Keep it updated and be careful about what you join, like, and share on your page. Put the privacy and security settings to where you must to approve what someone posts about you and whether or not you want it posted on your page and/or be tagged in it. The issue with social media is you don't control all of the content posted about you. When you do share or post something, make it uplifting and positive. Not too much of it. But a Share or Like of a video of cute puppies is infinitely better than you being tagged in a party photo someone else took and yet another posted, where the tagline of the photo is "Drunkfest 2016!!!"

- **Build your network:** The idea is that Facebook should be a way for you to connect and interact with others, but in a way that promotes you in a positive, uplifting way. Seems like common sense. But if you are on Facebook on a regular basis, you know that a lot of your "Friends" do not always use it in such a way.

However, your Facebook page is only the beginning. There are several other social media that are used by millions of people each day.

Twitter

That age-old 21st century question: *"To Tweet or Not to Tweet!?"* Twitter (twitter.com) is the social media that allows you to post a "tweet" containing no more than 140 characters. But Twitter is not just about what you tweet. While it is possible to block people, most people do not care (nor do they look carefully) at who is FOLLOWING them. Employers will not just look at your tweets, but they can discover what others are tweeting about you. In fact, what might be of interest to a potential employer is who you follow on Twitter, as well as who is following you. Our tips for Twitter, therefore, are quite simple:

- **Tweet with care:** Think about the words and images/videos/links you connect to your tweets. While you can delete a tweet, what if someone has re-tweeted it or clicked the "Print Screen" button on their keyboard? Your tweets can be permanent even if you delete them! Sometimes what you deleted will also be deleted for those who have re-tweeted it. But very often, this is not the case. So in a sense, things put out in cyberspace stay in cyberspace forever. Your digital fingerprint does not just reach those who you are "Friends" with or who follow you. Your digital fingerprint reaches an infinite audience, forever.

- **Think about who is following you:** While many consider it some type of competition to have as many Twitter followers as possible, you might want to block those who might not be considered the best for your reputation. Remember, those with Twitter accounts include not only individuals, but companies, organizations, causes, and ideas. Remember, you can and will be judged by those you follow and those followers – it's called *"guilt by association"*.

- **Think about who you are following:** You can learn a lot about a person based on who they follow on Twitter. Be careful that who or what you follow does not back you into that *"It does not matter how something is intended, it only matters how it can be taken"* trap. While you following Funny Animals Twitter account, some of the images might show animals being harmed. You saw a post once of a short video of a dog catching a Frisbee; but when your employer checks that account, they come across a posting of dogs being forced to fight each other for money (betting), because someone else out there thought it was funny. So just keep in mind, not everything is what it seems to be!

YouTube

YouTube (youtube.com) is not only a place to look at video content on anything from personal videos to local news to television shows or movies. While there are regulations and a few safeguards (like having to log in for content that is considered violent, for example), you should be aware of the following regarding your use of YouTube as social media.

- **Why YouTube is a social media:** While most people use it to simply view content, remember that YouTube is a social media because people can also interact (leave comments) on that video content.

- **Videos you upload:** Like any digital media, anything you upload or share should be done with great care. That company outing that involved a picnic and friendly soccer game that shows people who are intoxicated or a couple of co-workers getting into a heated argument about something goes viral for a reason: People love to watch other people making a fool of themselves. What does it say about you, when you upload such a video? What does it say if you are one of the people appearing in such a video?

- **Videos that you are in:** If someone else records a video involving you and it ends up on YouTube, there is little you can do to get it taken down other than ask them to do so.

- **Videos you respond to:** Any video on YouTube has a Comments section, where visitors to YouTube.com interact with one another. Be careful with what videos you respond to and what you write any time you do respond. You are never truly anonymous anywhere in cyberspace!

- **Your YouTube Channel:** Many people have their own YouTube account, where they can put up and show any number of their own or other videos. So again, the tip here is simply to be careful what you place on your YouTube channel. You are what you watch; you are what you share!

Instagram/SnapChat

Like any image-based social media, it really is all about managing what photos or videos you post and photos or videos posted of (or about) you. It's a matter of being careful with regards to two simple tips:

- **Photos/videos that you post:** Think about posting any photograph (on any social media). While you might later take it away, remember someone out there could take a screen shot, or "screen grab", of what you posted. So the idea here is simple: THINK before you upload!

- **Photos/videos posted about you:** Try and maintain every effort to be on top of this. Reject any posting of an image involving you (showing you or mentioning your name) that you think could be misunderstood or taken out of context. When you are not able to control or "approve/reject" any image of you or mentioning your name, take the time to politely contact the person who posted it and ask them to remove it (if it is a photo of you) or remove the tag that involves your name being a part of or associated with that image.

- **Security Settings:** Remember to set your security on settings on Instagram, as you can control who is following you on your account. You also have to "approve" connecting to someone on newer imaging apps like SnapChat.

Pinterest

After LinkedIn, it is recommended that you join Pinterest, for no other reason than that you can search for things like CV layout ideas or "Common questions in interviews" or "Tips on non-verbal communication" and find tons of tips and ideas.

Not everyone has a Pinterest account (pinterest.com) and if you don't, like nearly all social media, the concept is simple: Pinterest is just what it sounds like: It is a pin board or a digital bulletin board of your interests. You are, in fact, pinning up (or posting) your interests or hobbies. And yes, people can check up on and connect to (follow) what is on your bulletin board of interests. If you do use this social media (or might check it out after reading this), consider the following:

- **Tips on CVs & Careers:** Pinterest provides an infinite number of tips and ideas on designing your CV or resume. There are tips on interview questions, writing cover letters, and wardrobe ideas. There are pins on presentation techniques, public speaking, and non-verbal communication.

- **You ARE your interests:** When you "pin up" any number of possible topics that you are interested in, make sure you are posting items that would not be considered controversial or easily misunderstood. If we have said it once, we have said it a hundred times in this book: However you intend an interest for yourself to be (e.g. "shooting guns"), it can be interpreted by someone else in a completely different way.

- **Think about your PINS:** Are there pins that show your interests that could hurt your brand? Are there some that are missing that might help your brand? For example, you want to be hired at a company that has a large corporate focus on sustainability and the environment. As long as you sincerely share that interest, pin up a few recycling or "help the environment" pins on your page.

- **Pin your interests:** As in the previous tip, while Pinterest can allow you to pin your interests on many levels and areas, think along the lines that it is o.k. to pin your professional and personal interests, but beware anything that could be deemed too private. Try and keep your pins focused on Professional You (e.g. CV tips; Interview Tips & Questions) and Personal You (e.g. Cleaning Hacks for your Home; 5-ingredient Recipes). While many of us like to unwind with a beer or have a glass of wine with our dinner, a pin on "1001 Drink Recipes" could be interpreted that you like to drink a lot. We are not saying don't have such a pin – but realize how such a pin *could* be interpreted.

Blogs

Blogs are the 21st century version of having our own magazine; our own newspaper; our own outlet for letting the world know what we think at any given moment. For bloggers, the idea is to have an outlet that is not just a Facebook post or trying to make a point while limited to 140 characters on Twitter. Blogs exist on every topic imaginable. And we are judged on two things when it comes to this:

- **Do you write a blog?** If so, then anything and everything you write can either help Brand YOU or it can potentially hurt Brand YOU. Is your blog about you, a cause you believe in, or something that you have undertaken professionally (e.g. writing a blog for a company, an organization, or a student group while in college)? What words do you use and how do you express yourself? Is your blog an online journal of your life? Is your blog some sort of get-rich-quick scheme? Is your blog a happy, uplifting place? Or is it an outlet for your anger and the injustices you see in the world? Simply put, be careful what you blog about. More specifically, be careful how you phrase things in your writing. It might not any particular blog that becomes a potential problem. It might just be one, simple sentence in a single blog you posted over two years ago that comes back to haunt (or help) you.

- **What blogs do you follow, read or promote?** Do you comment on other people's blogs? Do you maintain a list or record (and share) what blogs you follow or read regularly? Do you often share or repost a blog on other social media such as Facebook or Twitter?

- **Are you mentioned in a blog?** You might not even be aware of this until you find a way to Google yourself. In fact, many people find their names being mentioned in blogs (or other websites) they never even knew existed. If you are a part of something that is even somewhat visible to the public, your name can be out there. This could be an organization you belong to or are a leader of; something you volunteer for; a cause you have lent your name to; an organization you are a member of; a project you were once a part of – and the list goes on!

- **Love vs. Hate:** Remember that every blogger, if they have built any sort of audience, invite and likely have both those who love what they write and those who hate or at least strongly disagree with what they write. In a democracy, all views are welcome. So don't react angrily or get too defensive against someone who disagrees with you on something. Keep it professional, no matter what.

Skype

We use Skype (skype.com) for both personal and professional reasons. In fact, more and more organizations are turning to Skype for interviewing job applicants, especially for that first interview or to keep in touch after the first interview. Remember that early scene from the 2013, Twentieth Century Fox film, "The Internship" starring Vince Vaughn and Owen Wilson? How they sat in a library being interviewed for that Google internship opportunity? While they did not use Skype for this online interview, the idea is the same for any computer, tablet or smart phone with a microphone and webcam. When it comes to Skype (or any type of voice-to-voice or face-to-face digital technology), we recommend:

- **Have your own Skype account:** If you are not on Skype yet, then start a Skype account now, so you are ready to go in case that potential employer wants to first "meet you" via this social media. Then use it to call others. Remember that Skype allows you to text chat, talk only (voice-to-voice), and video chat (face-to-face conversation) with others. Practice using Skype in all these forms and make sure your audio and video settings are all pre-set and saved.

- **You get what you pay for:** Most laptops and smart devices today come with decent, built-in video cameras and microphones. If not, or if the quality is not that good on your device, then invest in a good, high-def, 720p or 1080p video camera connected to your computer, as well as a decent headset that allows you to talk as well. If you do not use a desktop or laptop computer, think about the smart device (pad or phone) you buy, as you will have to connect it via the built-in camera and microphone that comes with those devices.

- **Your Skype name:** As with any social media or digital technology, think about your user name for social media like Skype and make it sound professional. Try and avoid using "student" in email (common, since many Skype names are in fact someone's email name). Avoid cute or controversial nicknames, regardless of their origin or intended meaning. Simply put, try and make your Skype name, like your email names, as professional as possible.

• Remember that very often, those personal and professional Skype text chats, voice-to-voice calls, and those face-to-face (video) phone calls can be recorded by someone; If not directly from the app, then from them holding up their smart phone camera to their computer monitor.

Any time you subscribe to or use any of the social media available today, it is an invitation for potential employers, competitors, or even your current co-workers to connect to you, follow you, or at the very least check up on you. Basically, it comes down to how you develop and manage what we consider to be your Professional vs. Personal social media (depending on how you use them).

Consider and do your best to stay on top of what you are posting, what others post about you, and remember to Google yourself once in a while. Beware of who you add to your list of Friends or Contacts, as well as who you interact with or respond to in any of these social media. Remember, *"You are who you associate yourself with!"* is a good way to look at it. It does not mean we can't have family members or friends who have had trouble in their life. It just means, think twice before responding to a request to connect or respond to someone within any social media.

Remember that social media should be about helping the PROFESSIONAL level of Brand YOU, even if it is something PERSONAL. And in general, with regards to cyberspace, and more specifically with regards to social media, there is no such thing as truly PRIVATE. Social means shared with and by others.

On the next page there are a few exercises for you to use in doing a true, social media audit on yourself.

Workbook – Chapter 9

Your digital presence stretches further than you may ever have realized. The exercises in this chapter are meant for you to conduct a review, discover what is out there, analyze your social media habits, "clean things up", and, most importantly, start or update your LinkedIn page. More specifically, consider the following exercises to get you started:

EXERCISE 9 A – Join LinkedIn.com today

- ESTABLISH or UPDATE your professional social media (LinkedIn)
- Begin to CONNECT to people you know who are on LinkedIn. The more contacts you have, the more you will grow your network and communicate your brand in the most professional online way possible.
- Link to the authors of this textbook for examples of how you can set up your LinkedIn page:
- TIM: linkedin.com/in/timfos
- MIA: linkedin.com/in/miaoldenburg

EXERCISE 9 B – Google yourself

- Google "Google yourself" or "How to Google yourself" and you will come across a myriad of links with tips on how to do this. This personal "Google Audit" should be done at least every 6–12 months to stay on top of just how your most valuable assets, your name and reputation, are being discussed and shared online. Remember, most organizations will Google you, so you need to do it as well.
- Really dig deep, using a combination of various search terms using your name. EXAMPLE: Most of us have fairly common names. So put your name (first name + last name) and connect it to something

specific. This could be Your Name, City; Your Name, employer; Your Name + organization you were involved in; etc.

- See what is out there about you, both personally and professionally.

EXERCISE 9 C – Evaluate your social media use

- Which social media do you use? Facebook, Twitter, Pinterest, Blogs, Instagram, Flickr, Snapchat, Skype, etc.?

- What does your use of each of your social media memberships say about you?

- What do you want to achieve with each of the social media that you are a part of?

- Go over your lists of friends, contacts and/or followers in each of the social media you use. Use a critical eye to ask yourself: is my association with this person helping or hurting me?

- Always check your security and privacy settings so that you maintain a higher degree of control and the chance to receive an "alert" when something is posted about you (a comment, photo, or video using your name or showing your image).

- Remove unwanted posts or tags involving you (or ask someone to do it if you don't have that capability).

- Continually monitor and think about what you are posting and what others are posting about you.

- Does this help or hurt Brand YOU?

- New social media appear all the time! Is it important that you are a part of all of them, or should you be more selective? While any of them can help communicate Brand YOU, none of them are 100% controlled by you or what is posted about you.

- Remember to be positive in all your postings!

CHAPTER 10

The End is Only the Beginning …

"Don't ask what the world needs, ask what makes you come alive and go do it. Because what the world needs are people who have come alive."

HOWARD THURMAN

The end of this book is only the beginning to the "New & Improved" Brand YOU. The aim of this book was to put you on a journey of self-discovery; a journey that has allowed you to focus on your strengths, but made you confront your weaknesses as well. Having a better understanding of yourself as a brand in a competitive marketplace will allow you to begin to focus on achieving your goals, many of which are focused on being able to compete in what has become a global marketplace for talent.

Organizations do not look only at the school you attended, the grades you achieved, the experience you have accumulated, or the skills you possess. They are looking for a PERSON. A person with a specific set of strengths, skills and personality traits that fits in with their organizational culture and objectives. You are in fact possibly being added to their pool of talent and, at the end of each day or week or month that you work for them, you help them create value.

Ask yourself, what is McDonalds without the Big Mac? What is Proctor & Gamble without Pampers diapers? What is Ford Motor Company without its Mustang? What is IKEA without its meatball lunches? Take away any of these brands from these corporate giants and they will probably all remain in business. But losing any of those brands from their respective organization would put them at a competitive disadvantage. Losing any of those brands would decrease their overall value as an organization.

What if the organization did not have you? If an organization truly values you, it is because you bring value to them. And losing you should be considered something that puts them at a competitive disadvantage. This should be true whether you are the CEO, a middle-level manager, a college student doing an internship, the secretary taking care of the administrative functions, or the person cleaning the offices at night, after everyone goes home. It is not enough that everyone in an organization represents the brand(s) they work for, but they themselves ARE a brand that adds value to the organization as a whole.

Organizations today are facing the cold, hard reality that is competitive hiring. They are moving away from filling jobs and functions and are instead focused on finding talent, strengths and most of all specific types of personalities. They are looking for the right kind of person, that human being with the education and experience required to get the job, but more importantly someone with the people and communication skills that does not just serve a particular need for the organization, but adds true value to that organization as a whole. And no matter what, you will face two predicaments when it comes to getting hired: Handling rejection and managing success.

Handling Brand YOU through rejection

Don't be afraid to fail. Failure should be seen as an invitation to learn and develop your personal brand. The simple truth is, we all get rejected. Let's get that out of the way and say it up front. Too often, we see rejection or not getting the job as a failure. H. Stanley Judd put it best:

> "Don't be afraid to fail. Don't waste energy trying to cover up failure. Learn from your failures and go on to the next challenge. It's o.k. to fail. If you're not failing, you're not growing."

Put another way, if you're not failing, then you're not trying!

This book, your CV, your interview skills – none of it guarantees you getting hired. You will be rejected more often than you will have offers. Some job openings can have several hundred or even several thousand applicants sending in or uploading their cover letters, CVs, and LinkedIn page. Today's 21st century, global economy that we all live in means there are more opportunities than ever before, each one with a larger number and higher degree of competition. But look at it this way as well: The world has, in fact, become your marketplace for finding work. Information technology, as it affects communication, transportation, and human interaction, will forever be the one factor that influences our careers.

Here are some common questions that people ask themselves that we refer to as "Tips when dealing with being rejected":

- *How should I handle rejection or simply not hearing from a potential employer?* Accept it as a learning experience and move on. It likely came down to the fact that they simply found someone they felt was more qualified and/or whose education, experience, and personality better fit what they were ultimately looking for. Let rejection strengthen your resolve to keep trying, keep finding ways to improve. Don't let rejection bring you down.

- *Why didn't I at least get the interview? Should I call or write them a letter or email demanding to know why?* Of course not. That will just eat up more of their time and show that you lack both the common sense and common courtesy to accept that it was (a) Not just you who was interested in the job opening; (b) Everything being equal (work, experience, skills, etc.), they simply decided to interview others.

- *If I have not heard from them, should I at least call to make sure they have received my CV?* Our recommendation, as explained in Chapter 7, is no. Don't do this. Trust that your cover letter and CV arrived safely. Then consider the potential volume of applications that came through. They need time to go through all of it. If you become a part of who they are looking for, they will contact you. Not hearing from them implies, quite simply, that you did not make it through to be considered for a first interview. And if you made it to the first interview but were not invited back for a second interview (or offered the job), it means the same thing: Not interested.

- However, just as we are rejected at times, we will also have the chance to taste the sweetness of success. For some, success is measured in developing their cover letter and CV enough to be asked in for a first interview. For others, it might be making it through to the small group of finalists for the position this time. Other times, it is measured in actually being offered the job, and you rejecting them. The ultimate is when you are offered the job and then choose to accept it.

- But what then? Isn't the ultimate action, the ultimate success for Branding YOU being offered and accepting that job you really wanted? What now? Now you have succeeded, but with that comes the need to focus a new strategy on managing your brand through this success.

Managing Brand YOU through success

But what if you get the job? Should you take it? What if something better comes along? Uncertainty often rears its ugly head when the job offer actually arrives. Second-guessing yourself is natural. However, every experience you take on in your life is adding a life lesson for you. As Stephen Kellogg once said, *"It is always better to be at the bottom of the ladder you want to climb than at the top of the one you don't."*

Look at it this way: Each experience you choose to add to your life will add to the value of Brand YOU. Some experiences are short-lived; others might feel like they will become a lifelong commitment or even a calling. Some experiences will be difficult to handle. Others will become a highlight of your life. Each and every one provides learning opportunities that, in the end, only strengthen and provide value to Brand YOU. In the end, remain humble, be nice, and listen more than you talk, and success will find you.

Just as you will be rejected, you will also find success. You will have job offers. Like in the movie "Dave"[1] with Kevin Cline, when talking about getting offered a job: *"Have you ever seen the look on somebody's face, the day that they finally get a job? … They look like they could fly … and it's not about the paycheck, it's about respect … it's about looking in the mirror and knowing you did something valuable with your day."* Well, dear reader, it's time to do

---

1 From the 1993 Warner Brothers movie "Dave" starring Kevin Cline and Sigourney Weaver.

just that. It's time to embrace the cliché *Carpé Diem – Seize the Day!* If you are offered and accept a job, embrace the success, and then realize that the real work lies ahead. You not only want to keep the job, but you want to find ways to advance, move up, and continue to challenge Brand YOU.

Once you are offered the job, think and communicate before you accept it. Once the job is offered, only then should you begin to discuss and negotiate important issues related to it, the most important of which, for most, involves how much you will be paid.

Knowing your options

Since this book focuses 80% on Professional You and 20% on Personal You, consider what options there might be for you to add value to other people's lives, instead of just your own, and in turn make such value creation a part of your career. Knowledge about employability and the needs of your target market (as presented in Chapter 4) are important. You need to know about your options: What is available for you out there in terms of optional job titles? Is there room for a new niche for Brand YOU that you can create for yourself? And as shown in Figure 10.1, where do you and your target market overlap?

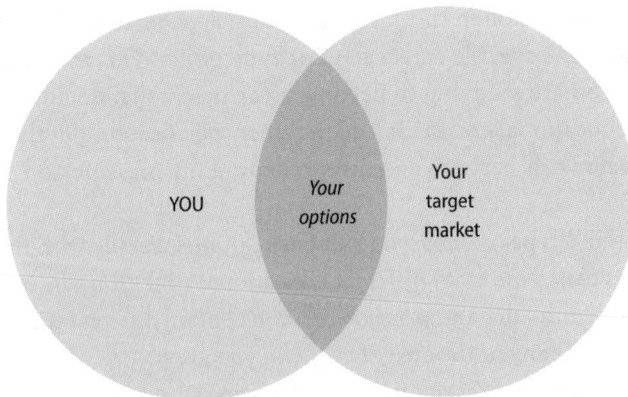

FIGURE 10.1 Your options – where you and your target market overlap.

We all know about people who, even just 30 years ago, did not even have to apply for a job. If they had the right educational background they just got a job without even having to go through an application process. That is not the case anymore. Jobs nowadays are so much more complex and changes within nearly all industries and most organizations are happening at a very fast pace. Companies are not hiring solely on education and qualifications anymore. More and more they are looking for the right personalities to enter their company and join their team. They are looking for people with the ability to grow and change with the company and the people already in it. So, be open to growth and be willing to change and keep your options open when applying for a new job. Organizations are, of course, looking for people with a certain education, skill set, and experience, but more and more they are looking for a set of personality traits – i.e. *the right person!*

When exploring your options, dare to think and dream big enough to look outside your comfort zone even though self-awareness also means being realistic about your options. You will notice people with the same educational background end up having all kinds of different job titles, as well as that people with the *same* job title come from different educational backgrounds.

So *what* you study is not really as important as *that* you study. Your education will get you a foot in the door but your *transferable skills* and *personal attributes* will get you ahead and shape your career, as outlined in Figure 10.2.

Many college students often think that a certain type of education or degree leads to just one specific career path or type of job. This might of course be true if you are studying to become a car mechanic, doctor, or nurse. There are educational areas that lead to rather specific jobs. But then again, even a doctor can become an entrepreneur, a business person, a manager, a CEO.

So even with those types of jobs, you still have options. People with the same types of jobs can come from different educational backgrounds. It is important to keep in mind that the same job title can contain different things depending on the company or the area of business you are in.

With this in mind there is absolutely no need to narrow down your list of possible job titles, or keep a list of jobs that is limited to what you think you must work with. Instead think more broadly about your future career choices and keep your options open. Adding your inner-dream and passions

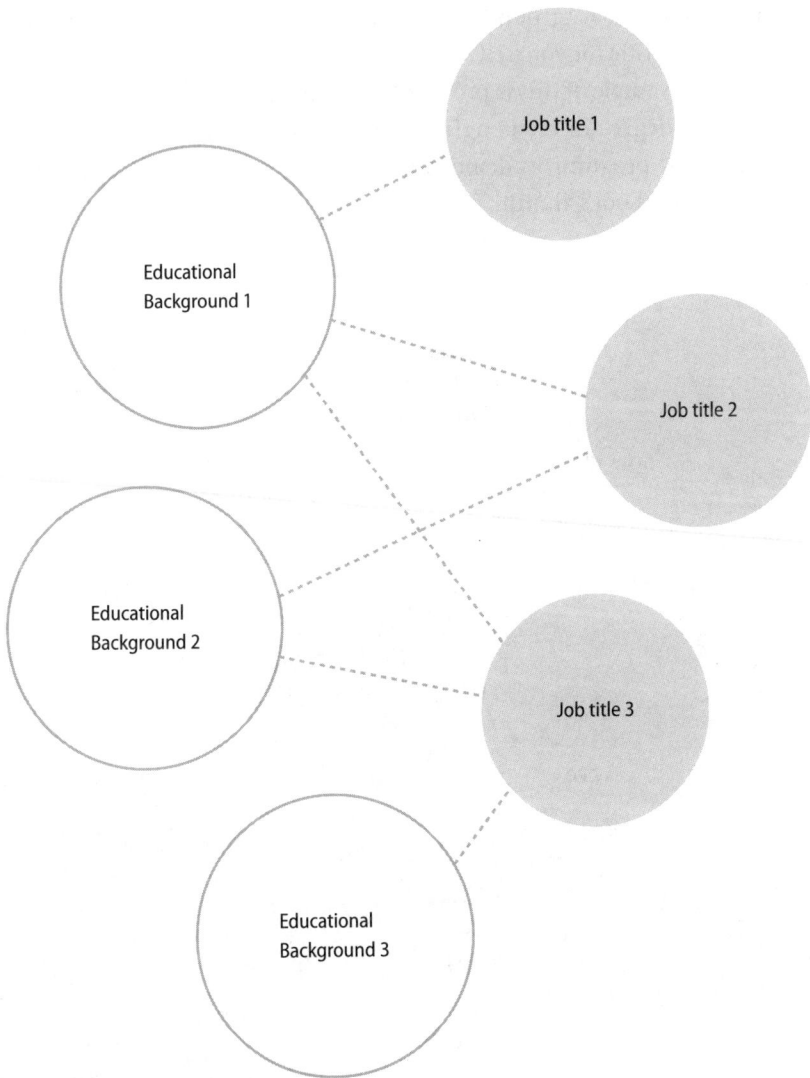

FIGURE 10.2 The same educational background can lead to several different jobs, just as different educational backgrounds can lead to the same job.

to your educational background can help you find your own niche or create a whole new job title for yourself.

An actual example of this is provided below in Figure 10.3. This example shows what a degree in civil engineering ended up meaning for several graduates of the program, as demonstrated by using LinkedIn to track the careers of your school's alumni.

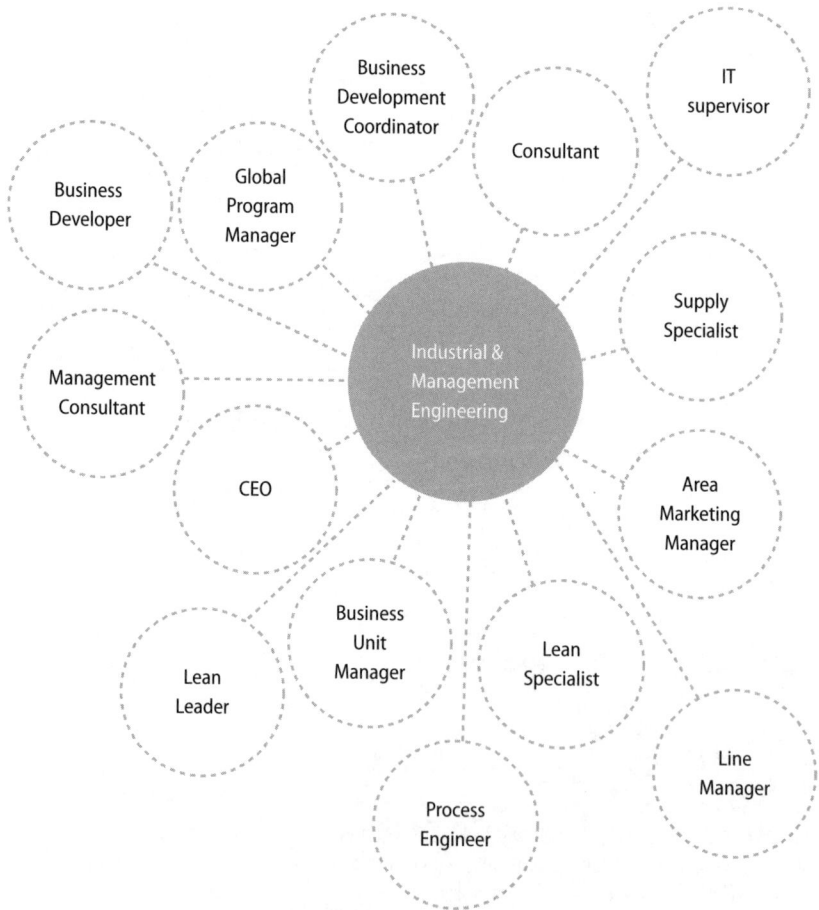

FIGURE 10.3 A range of different work titles for alumni from Industrial and management engineering programs at Luleå University of Technology, Sweden (SOURCE: LinkedIn, 2013).

With Figure 10.3 above only serving as an example, a degree in civil engineering can turn into any number of job opportunities or titles. It's not what the degree is in that counts, it is how you are able to use it throughout your career. And as your career progresses over the years and decades that will make up this working part of your life, your college (or other) degrees will mean less and less. As your career progresses, experience and your ever-expanding network will open more doors than education.

Organizations are looking for people with a 3-dimensional way of thinking – *creative, innovative* and *driven* no matter their educational background. It is not as important to be specialized now as it was in the 20th century. Today, communication and people skills are higher on the list. Your ability to learn and listen to others, as well as your being interested and able to connect to others are actually the attributes most valued by organizations today.

To increase your employability you need to challenge yourself every day, push yourself outside your comfort zone and force yourself to grow and develop, without judging too harshly the mistakes you make along the way. Learn from your mistakes, but don't let them become the anchor around your neck that keeps you from moving forward, from making progress. See mistakes as invitations to learn!

Here is an example to illustrate this:

Melissa is really interested in a job opportunity that will require her to make presentations in front of both small and large groups of people. As illustrated in Figure 10.4, this is a bit outside Melissa's comfort zone.

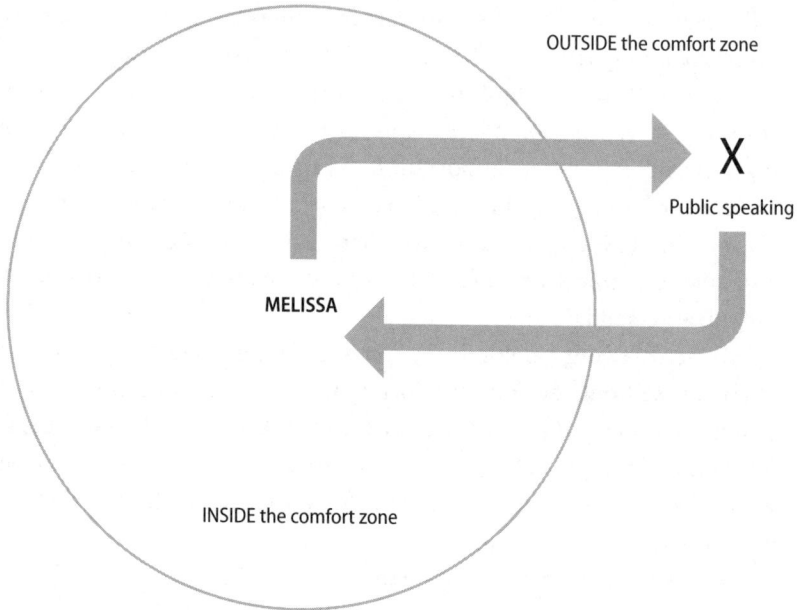

OUTSIDE the comfort zone

X

Public speaking

MELISSA

INSIDE the comfort zone

FIGURE 10.4 What is inside and outside your comfort zone.

Melissa has two options if she is serious about applying for this job (as illustrated by the arrows in Figure 10.4): She needs to put the time in to practice and improve her public speaking and making presentations in front of others, helping to move her from outside her comfort zone to inside her comfort zone; OR she needs to be "o.k." with how it feels to be outside her comfort zone at times while performing the duties of the job. And for nearly all of us, staying inside our comfort zone might be what is easiest, but real progress and opportunity happen when we are willing to go outside it once in a while.

Negotiating your salary

You will never get what you deserve or think you are entitled to; you will only get what you bargain for. You need to impact the employer and look at mutual interests and seek to create value for both of you. Look at the objective criteria: What do you offer and how is that valuable for your employer? How can they reimburse you for creating that value for them? You are trading your work for their pay but they can pay you in a lot of different ways that indirectly translate into money.

Remember it's not all about the money and benefits, although that's important too. What else is there to gain from a job beyond money and other benefits? What more should you consider before walking away from a job offer just because to pay is too low for your standards? These factors are often overlooked but actually more important to your future career than the size of you paychecks early in your career:

- **Network**: Will this job offer me a great network within my desired industry that will be valuable for me in the future?

- **Experience**: Will this job give me the experience I need to get ahead in my career?

- **Qualification**: Will this job give me the qualifications that are necessary for me to take the next step forward later on?

- **References**: Will it give me references needed when I apply for a job in the future?

Sometimes getting your foot in the door at the right place will give you so much opportunity later on that it can become more valuable than money will ever be. A couple of examples help to illustrate this:

Minna really wanted to work within television and she realized early on that she needed to start from scratch and work her way up in that very competitive industry that lets no one take shortcuts. So although she had a university degree within the industry she started as an assistant, helping out with everything from running errands, making lunch for the people on set and driving them around. She was always friendly and hard working so for the next project she was asked to take on another role in the team. Gradually she climbed higher and higher and after a few years she had gained not only the experience but also a great reputation as hard working and nice and was given the chance to be the producer at a large TV event.

Viktor was moving from a large city to a smaller one where he had no network. He applied for and was offered a job well below his qualifications. However, the job was within a large organization and he started to grow his network and look for opportunities inside the company. After a few years he could look back at a great career, changing ranks every other year.

The moral of these stories is that it does not matter where you start, it only matters what steps you take after that. You need to start somewhere, but you do not have to remain (nor are you likely to remain) in the same entry level position forever.

Negotiating salary is a stressful situation and people tend to not prepare themselves enough for such an important issue. There are so many variables to consider before entering a salary negotiating situation. Some of the more important ones include:

1. Research ahead of time the salary levels and benefits of the specific industry. Is what they are offering below, the same, or above this?

2. Research the specific company and the specific job title for salary levels and benefits.

3. Their expectations and requirements on you – what level of responsibility will they ask of you? What are the hours you are expected to put in?

4. What does the market look like at the moment? Is the company doing well or having problems (financial or otherwise)? Is your competence in high demand or are you competing with several others that have similar competencies?

5. Think of a range (monthly or annual salary), not an exact amount. Your aim or hope is that your range of salary somehow overlaps with the range in salary they were willing to offer when they offered you the job and/or began to negotiate your salary with you.

You need to take control and prepare, and stay away from traps of getting emotional, taking a harsh stand, demanding, claiming and arguing. That will definitely get you nowhere. Think of it this way regarding negotiating your salary: Around 80% of the time should be used to prepare for the salary negotiation (i.e. do your homework); 20% should be dedicated to the actual negotiating.

Harvard Business School runs the Harvard Negotiating Project.[2] What this research shows is that the cornerstones in any negotiating situation is that if you ask for what you want, and tell people what you are interested in, it's usually easier to get it.

So, being quiet about what you want will not get you anywhere, but playing hardball will not get you what you want either. If your only focus revolves around what you yourself can gain and does not consider your employer's interests, you will not get ahead either. You need to have an interest in what the employer wants to have a successful negotiation for both of you.

Listen to them, be responsive to their needs. Be honest and transparent about your needs. Then think about the idea that "True Value" is when both sides consider what each side puts in (gives up) and what each side gains (takes out) of establishing this employer-employee value-creating relationship (see figure 10.5).

---

2 AVAILABLE: www.pon.harvard.edu/research_projects/harvard-negotiation-project/hnp/ (ACCESSED: June 25, 2016); or just Google "Harvard Negotiation Project".

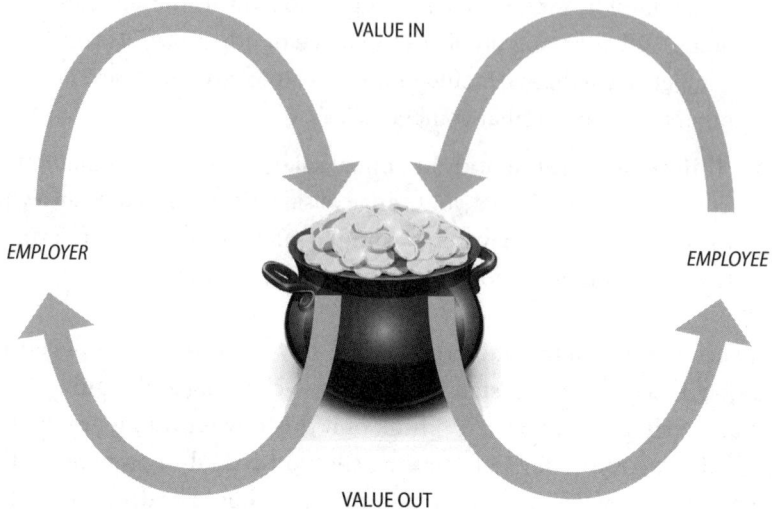

FIGURE 10.5 Creating Employer/Employee Value.

It comes down to understanding and then creating a win-win situation. It is often easier to negotiate benefits related to the job than it is to negotiate a higher salary. Based on Figure 10.5 above, here are some things to consider regarding what each side puts in, and what they take out of this employer-employee value-creating relationship:

VALUE IN:

- The EMPLOYER provides the job opportunity; salary; taxes to bring you on as an employee; possible benefits (medical insurance, dental coverage, life insurance); advancement and networking opportunities; tangible items such as coffee or lunches, or what about travel, an office, a phone, a computer or a car.

- The EMPLOYEE offers the experience and education needed to obtain such a job; they bring through this education and experience the knowledge, skills and abilities to do the job; they bring the network that they have already built; the employee gives up their time to contribute towards that organization achieving results.

VALUE OUT:

- The EMPLOYER takes out what is listed under Value In for the employee above.
- The EMPLOYEE takes out those items listed under Value In for the employer above.

Overall, it is recommended that you find out what it is that is easy for them to give you and bake that into your requests. An example would be if you worked for a bank: Is it possible for them to provide a mortgage loan with a lower interest rate? Another example: If you work for a university, do they allow employees time to attend their courses during working hours (and in some parts of the world at a lower or no-tuition rate)?

Turn this into quantitate numbers to back up your salary requests. Package your services, describe how you can contribute and the benefits and value they provide for the company. Maybe you have a specific skill, knowledge or experience that adds quality to their business that they did not have before. Turn all of this into arguments to support your requests.

Here are some suggestions on what you also can negotiate:

- **Time**: What *are* the working hours? Do they offer flexible hours? Do you have to check-in for them to keep track of your hours or is it the type of job where your work hours are up to you? Will you be able to go to the gym or the doctor during working hours? Do they compensate for overtime?

- **Quality**: What is the size and location of your office? Do they provide office furniture, computer, phone, office supplies, etc.? Are there opportunities to work partly from home? Are there opportunities to attend courses and conferences? Will you be able to travel? Is the travel local, regional, national or international in nature? Are there health benefits, dental plans, childcare, interest-free/low-interest loans? Will you have an expense account or any type of assistance or allowance for clothing? What are the networking opportunities with this job?

- **Quantity**: Your monthly salary? How many vacation days? Are there any types of profit-sharing options, employee stock options or bonuses? How much is your expense account?

Make sure you look at all these factors as well as the salary itself, because all of this is money too. What are the unwritten expectations? What is the norm on these factors for your industry? Is what they offer adequate for what they expect of you and what value you bring to the table? Are employees expected to come in to the office every Sunday?

As has been pointed out, the market will have a big influence on your salary, as will your individual success and experience from within the organization or from another organization you are coming from.

Put yourself in your employer's shoes for a while. The example below involves **Rob,** who was brought into a service business to add to the bottom line, make the organization more profitable, and provide his unique set of management and leadership skills:

"I was hired by a service organization in the healthcare industry. I was on the fast-track to become partner, and when I did become a partner, I soon became involved in managing the organization. This included but was not limited to the hiring of employees at all levels. Once hired, each employee took part in an annual performance review, but these same questions below applied to hiring new employees as well. When someone was asking for a raise during these situations, my mindset was based on a series of questions, the answer to which needed to be yes on the majority of them: What do you offer/what have you brought (will bring) to our organization? Are we (will we be) better off after hiring you, compared to your not being here now? Are we more effective (i.e. reaching organizational objectives) or more efficient (i.e. using our resources) now than we were before we hired you? Are you doing what we asked you to do, or are you finding ways to exceed expectations? Every year we set work plan goals for the entire organization as well as for individual employees. Every year we develop an agreed management incentive plan and employee incentive plan that high-lights and quantifies elements of the work plan, with an escalating bonus structure for meeting certain thresholds. Thus, managers and employees are all "rowing in the same direction" to help achieve our primary work plan and financial goals every single year."

So salary negotiating is usually done *after* you have been offered a job. Even if the employer asks you to specify your salary requirements in your application, try and avoid doing this. Firstly, before you know their expectations, the conditions of the job, the level of responsibility and what benefits there are how could you possibly know what to ask for? Secondly you do not want them to disregard your application due to your requirements. A negotiation is not done by you specifying a number in your application. If you need to write anything in your application just write that salary is negotiable.

As Bolles (2010)[3] puts it: The best time for you to negotiate is not when they are still asking, *"Who are you?"* (i.e. at the first interview). Not even when you get the idea that they like you, or even "love you" (call you in for a second and even third interview). Until they have decided that they *"must have you,"* and you receive an offer, it is generally considered to be too early to negotiate salary. When you have an offer on the table, then and only then can you start to negotiate.

And make damn sure you have done your homework and prepared well by then, because once you start the job and realize that everyone is making more than you, you are too late. They got you already! So a strategy to avoid answering questions about your salary requirements before you actually got an offer is to ask them instead about the responsibility level and conditions of the job.

Try to avoid answering questions about your current salary that have nothing to do with another job, unless the expectations and responsibility level is as high AND if the industry is completely the same AND the market is the same for your competence AND if the companies' finances are the same. Only then will that question be of relevance.

Three steps for salary negotiation

So, they feel they must have you and you are now in a great bargaining position. The employer wants to hire you. They are already visualizing you at the office, dreaming about the value you will bring and the problems

3 Bolles, R. (2010). *What Color is Your Parachute? A Practical Manual for Job-Hunters and Career-Changers.* Berkely: Ten Speed Press.

you will solve for them. They do not want to lose you in the negotiating process. At this point they want you to love them back as much as they love you. However, they might be good at negotiating and have complete stone faces. Do not let this scare or intimidate you. It is, in fact, their job to keep salary expectations low and costs at minimum. Follow these three steps when negotiating your salary:

- STEP 1: Do your homework on the industry, company and the position you are applying for.

- STEP 2: Decide on a range that you think is reasonable considering the market for your competence, the salary levels that are the norm in the industry and their expectations of you. Also take into consideration other conditions and benefits and the value of those. What are standard and what can you include in your negotiation? What are your arguments to reach the higher end of your range? What is the lowest offer you can accept? What number are you really aiming for, and remember that you need to snap up to make room for them to negotiate it down. The number you are aiming for should be in the middle part of your range, not at the top end.

- STEP 3: Try not to be the first to specify a range. When they offer you the job make sure you show how excited you are but also ask them to specify the range they think is reasonable for the position. Since you have already done your homework you will know if that is indeed reasonable and you have your arguments ready as to why you should be on the higher end of their range. But do not forget to negotiate benefits as well.

If you are not at all on the same page, just remember that arguing, playing hardball or making harsh stands is not going to do you any good. In fact it could even make them take the offer back completely. You need to create a positive atmosphere and maintain a good relationship even though you do not like their offer(s). It's not about winning or losing, it is about trading values with each other, and you should keep your emotions in control at all times. Just let them know, in a nice way, that you were thinking more along the lines of range X to Y, hoping to fall somewhere in the middle of that range. And that you are asking for this amount due to your experience or knowledge in the areas needed for the job.

Then wait for their reaction.

Maybe they were just trying to get you really cheap or maybe their offer is really all they are willing to offer or can afford to pay. However, you won't know this until you make your point. Also ask about their range, how did they come up with those numbers and what would the benefits include? Never rush through this situation. Instead, lay low and take your time. You can easily afford a bit of friendly silence and hesitation, which might get them to take action to try to convince you and in doing that they might move their offer up a little bit at a time. If their offer is final, ask for time to think about it and make sure you check when it is you need to give them a final answer by.

Just remember, when you are at any job, collect your "success stories" of what value you created for the company and present them at your yearly salary review to answer their question – i.e. what have you done for me lately? What do you deliver? How do you interact, build and maintain relationships with customers, partners and coworkers? How are you being paid, praised and appreciated for the work you do and the results you deliver? Remember, they are paying you for results more than anything else! What have you achieved this year? What were the tangible results (i.e. the benefits for the employer/customer/partners)? What are your suggestions for how to improve on these results in the future?

One last thing: a lot of research shows that when you are paid enough to take the issue of money off the table, the really important factors in a job arise: That the job has a sense of purpose, is challenging, allows for mastery of certain skills, provides autonomy and self-direction, and allows you to make a solid contribution. So what you should really try to find is not the highest-paying job but a job that you are passionate about and the employer who offers you this.

The end is only the beginning

As you complete this book, you have hopefully taken the time to work with the exercises included at the end of most of the chapters. Each exercise has provided a means for providing you with a better understanding and opportunity for development of Brand YOU. If you have not really taken the time to do the exercises, then go back to each chapter and look them over one more time. Maybe there are a few you will find it worthwhile to work on. Choose those that appeal to you and do what that exercise is asking you to do. It is a way for you to get to know yourself as a brand, set goals for yourself as a brand, and learn to develop the strategies necessary to communicate your personal brand.

As a competitive bundle of strengths, skills and talents that must overcome certain weaknesses and threats that you face on a daily basis, it is important to realize that none of us are perfect. We never will be. But you are a brand. YOU will be that forever, as long as there are those around to remember you, even when you are gone. We call that a legacy. And beyond the practical elements that this book has offered for you to consider, what you leave behind yourself in the "wake of life" really ends up being about something more than just you: It's about how your life impacts the lives of others, both in terms of Professional You and Personal You.

The aim of this book is *not* for you to completely reinvent yourself. Focusing on yourself as a "brand" is really about you learning about whom you truly are and how this collection of strengths and weaknesses that make up your personality will allow you to begin to find a way for any number of possible employment opportunities awaiting you out there in the world. But it all depends on how you use your time.

We are each given a gift, and this gift is the only thing that makes us, as human beings, the same. It is the gift that follows what is referred to as:

The Law of 24

The Law of 24 states: *"The only thing that makes us equal as human beings is that we each get 24 hours a day. The only thing that makes us different is how we choose to use those 24 hours."* (Tim Foster)

There are no exceptions, no matter who you are, where you are from, what your culture, beliefs or practices are. The Law of 24 applies to us all. Each human being on planet earth gets 24 hours per day. That's it. Some are born with more opportunities than others. Some parts of the world are more or less free than others. Regardless of circumstances that we are born into or that we face today, we each still only get 24 hours each day. Use them wisely. Use them for good.

The Law of 24 asks some fairly simple questions: When you wake up tomorrow morning, what do YOU want to do? How will you get up and seize the day? How do you usually use your 24 hours per day? What will you do for the next 24?

You have to make a conscious choice to do something other than sit home and hope that something comes to you. Time to use your next 24 hours (and each of those that follow) more constructively in building the most important brand you will ever invest in: *A brand called YOU.*